The
Backside
of
Normal

The Backside of Normal

Normal: "Living According to What is Expected"
A Sailing Life of Adventure Takes Priority

by
Roger Olson

SEAWORTHY PUBLICATIONS, INC. ● MELBOURNE, FLORIDA

The Backside of Normal
Normal: "Living According to What is Expected"
A Sailing Life of Adventure Takes Priority.

Copyright ©2021 by Roger Olson

Published in the USA and distributed worldwide by:
Seaworthy Publications, Inc.
6300 N. Wickham Rd
Unit 130-416
Melbourne, FL 32940
Phone 310-610-3634
email orders@seaworthy.com
www.seaworthy.com

Library of Congress Cataloging-in-Publication Data

Names: Olson, Roger, 1939- author.
Title: The Backside of normal : a sailing life of adventure / By Roger Olson.
Description: Melbourne, Florida : Seaworthy Publications, Inc., [2021] |
  Summary: "For most of his life, Roger Olson tried to fit into the
  "so-called" American Dream. He got a master's degree in Education and
  taught high school for 15 years. He got married and tried to have
  children, then an unexpected divorce shattered his world and made him
  take stock of the life he was living. He needed to own a home that was
  close enough to his work, so he was saddled with a mortgage. He needed
  vehicles to get to and from work, and of course, these things lead to
  needing other things, like fuel, maintenance costs, insurance,
  electricity, and much more. Instead, Roger Olson went a different way.
  He managed to buy a small seaworthy sailing vessel, eventually quit his
  job and spent several decades sailing all over the Pacific, visiting
  many South Pacific island archipelagos, Australia, New Zealand, the
  Solomon Islands, Papua New Guinea, and Thailand. He is the author of the
  book, "Plot Your Course to Adventure: How To Be a Successful Cruiser" He
  is also the producer of the short film about his voyage entitled
  "Melanesian Adventure," now available on youtube.com"-- Provided by
  publisher.
Identifiers: LCCN 2020039031 (print) | LCCN 2020039032 (ebook) | ISBN
  9781948494427 (paperback) | ISBN 9781948494434 (epub)
Subjects: LCSH: Sailing. | Yachting. | Olson, Roger, 1939- | High school
  teachers--United States.
Classification: LCC GV811 .O47 2021 (print) | LCC GV811 (ebook) | DDC
  797.124--dc23
LC record available at https://lccn.loc.gov/2020039031
LC ebook record available at https://lccn.loc.gov/2020039032

Contents

Introduction

For most of his life, Roger Olson tried to fit into the "so-called" American Dream. He received a master's degree in education and taught high school for 15 years. He got married and tried to start a family. But then an unexpected divorce shattered the dream and made him take stock of the life he was living.

Even as a child, Roger never felt he was "normal," or "like everyone else." He would sit on the cliffs overlooking the Pacific Ocean and ponder what was on the other side of the horizon. He knew there was so much out there to see, and he wanted to see it, to be part of it, whatever it was. Roger dreamed of sailing to distant shores and reveled in stories he read about other sailors who had already made such voyages.

Roger owned and sailed a lot of different boats gaining the experience he would need and learning the lessons boat owners get to learn, usually the hard way. He went through several boats before he eventually found an ocean-going vessel that he could sail alone to any part of the world he wanted. Known as a Bristol Channel Cutter, Roger bought an unfinished hull at a fraction of the cost of a finished version, then worked on finishing the interior. He knew he was skilled with his hands and could manage the project himself. He also knew he could always find ways to earn more money to keep things going. Living on a small 28-foot sailboat can be as expensive or inexpensive as a person wants it to be. Roger would use this singular advantage to see the world.

"I have never known such fulfillment as cruising. I have visited places you cannot visit without a boat. I have adapted to various cultures, cooked, and eaten their food, and even lived according to their customs for short periods of time. There have not been any two days alike since I departed the States. I have new friends from all over the world. You must admit that it is an inexpensive way to live. And yes, there is some danger involved and accidents do happen."

This is his story, but to set the scene appropriately, it is important to understand that at the time Roger started on a voyage across an ocean with a newfound love interest in tow, at that time there was no GPS with point and click navigation to any part of the world. Voyages across oceans were navigated with a hand-held sextant and sight reduction tables. That fact alone was a barrier for many people venturing very far offshore. Once at sea, you were truly at the mercy of the elements since clear skies and calm waves were needed to get good sightings. Without good readings, vessels proceeded on dead reckoning which is only an estimate of headway. Therefore, some vessels, absent a good reading for too long, might end up in peril. Making landfall in those days was much the same as it was for the early explorers. They knew it was there, they just had to find it, and when sailors made landfall it was a cause for celebration.

Now let us hear Roger's story as he takes us on a journey across oceans to foreign lands and cultures. Let us see through his eyes and hear his thoughts about the world as it appeared to him. Let us experience his story and read about a life worth living.

Prologue

Well, here I am, 80 years old, having lived a life that is different than 99% of the people in the world. Every time I walk down my hallway and look at all the photos I have hung on the wall of the places I have been and the things I have seen, it brings back so many memories that I think others would be interested in knowing how I spent most of my life.

Many of my photos bring back good memories but there are a few that bring back some bad or sad ones. Well, that is all a part of the life I chose. After all, when a person decides to sail a small, 28-foot boat to distant places, he must accept there may be bad times as well as good ones. I accepted the possibility that my life could end in a storm at sea, being hit by a ship, or some other unexpected event in a strange place.

All my photos and artifacts make me smile because they are of old friends I made along my way. Some of the photos are of natives in their custom dress in Papua New Guinea, Vanuatu, and even Burma as well as other such island countries that I visited. I wonder if the "Long Neck" women in Burma still wear those rings around their necks that can make their neck up to ten inches long. They said they were going to stop that custom. I wonder if they did…

When I enter our second bedroom, the first thing I see on the walls are spears, bows and arrows, and primitive weapons that are still used in tribal wars. On other walls, there are more large photos of the natives of Papua New Guinea. My bookshelf does not have many books because I have it filled with perfect carvings that have "mother of pearl" shell pieces inlaid into the wood that is the same design as the tattoos they had on their faces. I even have a penis gourd that was the only thing the small *Nambors* wore when I was in Vanuatu. One shelf is full of shell money and stone money that they used in the Solomon Islands to buy brides and trade for items. I wonder if they still use this type of money for bargaining. There are so many items that I pick up and hold, each one brings back a clear memory of how I first got it.

My little condo is too small for me to have so many photos and artifacts all over the place. My wife does not appreciate any of it and if she had her way, they would all be thrown into the trash. I try to explain to her that they have such strong memories for me, that I could never get rid of them. She seems to acquiesce, but I know she does not understand that I lived a life that some would consider strange, and that these items really mean a lot to me. I know she would prefer we have normal things on display. After all, the things I have gathered during my lifetime have no memories for her. As a compromise, I removed anything of my past in our living room and bedroom.

My wife is from Colombia and does not speak a word of English, so we communicate using my poor Spanish. Though interestingly, when she is mad, I cannot understand a word she says. I turn my back on her and say, "si mi amor." This always settles things for the time being. I love her and I am sure she loves me too. We have been married for 15 years now. It has not always been easy, but I <u>think</u> we are both happy.

When I look back at my life, I realize I tried to live a normal life like everyone else and do what people expected of me. That did not make me happy. My dream was to see places and people one could only really see and visit with a small boat. No, my life was not normal, but I would not change a single thing I have done because this is what has made me who I am today. And, I like who I am and the life I lived.

I do not mention most people by their real names because I do not have their permission. Many have died. Others, I do not know how to contact them. I have had and still have some great friends that I would like to have mentioned and you will know if I wrote about you.

At the end of my writing, I have included the actual names of those to whom I am grateful because they have had a major positive influence on my life. I simply do not mention why.

If there is anything that I have learned in my many years on this earth, it is that compassion, forgiveness, and understanding for all people and living creatures are more important than anything else. There is a lot of prejudice in this world. A person is not born with prejudice, it is learned. When you meet someone who is prejudiced, you should ask them to explain, in detail, why they feel the way they do. I want the world to know that all cultures, whether primitive, of a different religion, a different color, or language; they all share the same feelings we do. They have the same emotions, sadness, fears, joys, compassion, and love. The only real difference is they may have a different skin color, have a different God, live a little differently than we do, or speak a different language. However, we are all the same in our hearts and feelings. Unfortunately, all cultures, races, and religions have some bad people, but they are generally in the minority, and one should never judge another culture just because they are different than us.

Chapter 1
A Life Change

Divorce: *My life is devastated because I never expected it and I loved my wife.*

*A*t the time, I was very busy teaching and attending a University at night to get my master's degree. My wife and I agreed that we would have children as soon as I got my master's and I could spend more time at home.

Late one Saturday night, my wife, who was an excellent typist, was typing the final pages of my master's thesis for me. Just as she typed the last period, I wanted to celebrate. I knew this was the last step to getting my master's degree, so I had bought two bottles of good champagne. I was pouring our first glass when, out of nowhere, she told me she wanted a divorce. She explained that she was in love with a counselor in the school where she was working. This tore me apart. I did not want the divorce, but I had no choice. I finished both bottles of champagne alone.

I tried everything I could to change her mind. She even agreed to give it a go for a month or so to see how she felt. After about a month, I asked her if she was happy now. She responded that she was still in love with the other man and needed more time to think about it. That was when I made the decision.

I filed for the divorce. We agreed to split everything we had. We had bought some investment property in Tehachapi that I gave back to the broker. I gave our house to a fellow teacher who only had to take over the payments. I was deeply hurt and simply wanted it all behind me. I walked away from many thousands of dollars. I just wanted to get on with my life. At that point, I swore I would never marry again.

I submitted my finished master's thesis and got my master's degree amid all this divorce turmoil.

My adjustment to being single was not easy. I shared an apartment with a fellow teacher who was about ten years my senior. He was having a difficult time going through his divorce as well. It seemed his divorce would be on then it was off. He said he had to get away from it all for a while. This echoed my feelings, so we decided to drive to Acapulco, Mexico during our summer vacation.

We stayed in cheap Mexican hotels where there were only Mexicans staying. Every night and many afternoons we would find a local Mexican cantina and drink tequila with the locals. Our Spanish was worse than horrible, but we managed. What little I learned certainly paid off many years later.

We discovered a local type of wine named *pulque*. It is a fermented drink, like wine, made from the same cactus plant used to make tequila. It did not taste bad and it was strong and cheap. We ended up drinking *pulque* nearly every day. We visited many places including Mexico City and the Mayan pyramids.

When we arrived in Acapulco, we stayed in a cheap hotel and spent most of our time on the beach during the day and in the bars at night. One night we met a couple of young American women who showed some interest in both of us. They would not go to our room with us but instead wanted to go for a night swim.

We left the bar and walked to the beach. My friend took off walking in a different direction with one of the girls. The other one, who stayed with me, began to undress. I saw she was wearing a swimsuit, so she had planned to go swimming earlier.

It was past midnight, so I took off my clothes except for my shorts. There was a small island or big rock only about 50 yards from shore. I figured we could swim out there, find shallow water, stand on the sand bottom, and make out or at least see what would happen where no one could see us.

She was a faster swimmer than me, so she got there first. I told her to try to touch the bottom and she let out a scream, then another and another. I thought something had bitten her and did not know what to do. She swam right at me, and then past me. I thought something was after her so we both swam as fast as we could toward shore. It was too dark to see any blood in the water and I was sure something was going to bite one of us at any second.

We made it to shore and began looking for cuts and blood flowing, but in the dark, we could see nothing, but she kept screaming with pain. We had to get her into some light, but she could not walk. My friend and his lady friend heard us and came running. He had a flashlight, so we searched for the cause of her pain. We saw a bunch of black spots on her feet, ankles, and knees.

She had stepped on sea urchins. The spines had entered her flesh and broke off at the surface. I know there is not much that can be done. You cannot pull them out because they have edges preventing them from going in a different direction. Once in, they can only be surgically removed. I showed her where I had hit the back of my hand and knee against a sea urchin once while diving for abalone. It looked like a black magic marker dot and hurt for months.

They said they wanted to find their husbands so they could go to the hospital. Husbands? It was apparent that they did not want us to go with them. We headed back to our room and had a few shots of tequila before going to bed. The next day we headed back to California.

Now that I was single, I began dating, but I did not want anything too serious. I swore I would never get married again. I was fortunate to have many short-term relationships. The major problem was that I had too many occasions where my female friend thought she might be pregnant.

This made me seriously think about having children someday. I gave it a lot of thought and so I began asking various female and male friends to seriously think about why they wanted children. I even asked those who had children, why they did it. When I heard their responses, they were mostly selfish answers. Most were the kind of answers you would hear from someone who wanted a pet. They wanted someone to love and love them back. Others wanted to have something they both could share, that would be part of them both. Then some just wanted to see what they could create. Some wanted to be sure their genes were carried on to future generations. Those who already had children said they would never have changed their minds and that they cherished their children. Each person had an answer; many were different, but none seemed to apply to me.

One of my favorite subjects in college was Philosophy which affected the decisions I made for the rest of my life. This philosophical background now kicked in to make the decision. I began to feel I was not like everyone else. I did not know what I wanted out of life, but I certainly did not feel that I had to have a child for any of the reasons I was given. If I found someone who already had children, that would be alright, but I felt no need to create my own. Even better, we could choose to adopt a child who needed a home. So, at the age of 34, I had a vasectomy and have since never regretted it.

At this time in my life, I let my religious beliefs drift away. I had been so badly hurt by the divorce and my philosophical mind questioned what, if anything, I wanted to do with my life.

Chapter 2
Becoming a Sailor

*N*early everyone who falls for the dream of sailing ends up going through a series of boats as they plan, think, and daydream about the future. Usually, each boat is, in one way or another, a steppingstone of both experience and knowledge, eventually leading to a fully formed notion of the right combination of boat, knowledge, and experience. Some reach a plateau beyond which, for one reason or another, they never exceed. My dream was to cross oceans, but to reach that point, I had to think in terms of total self-sufficiency on the world's oceans. But like most people, I went through a learning curve of sorts because to cross oceans there is a lot to know. All great dreams and journeys must begin with several small steps and falls until one day we know enough to be able to touch our dreams.

My First Boat: *Peace of Junk. I had no idea what I was doing but I learned how to sail and enjoy it because this was the beginning of the rest of my life.*

Now that I was single and had no responsibilities, I did not know, for sure what I wanted out of life. I still wondered what was over the ocean's horizon. I knew I loved the sea and I also liked women. So, I wanted both. I needed a magnet that would attract women and put me on the sea. I could buy a cheap, small boat. I did not want a powerboat because they consumed too much fuel. So, I wanted a sailboat, but I did not know how to sail. One day, I found this 30-foot, all teak, wooden, original Chinese junk that had been shipped from China. The way I had it figured, this unusual boat would attract women.

I went in partners with my roommate but soon discovered I was doing all the work and he was doing nothing. So, after the first six months, I bought him out for about half what he had invested.

I originally bought the boat to meet women but instead I found that I spent all my time working on it instead. So, there were no women in my life at that time. Slowly, I rebuilt the exterior, above the hull, and the interior of the boat. Not knowing what I was doing, I put wallpaper on the bulkheads (walls) and some sandbags in the bilge because a Chinese Junk does not have a ballast or lead weights to help keep the boat from leaning over too much in the wind.

I cast the name "PEACE OF JUNK" in bronze using a Chinese looking font. I also had a yellow sail made with a red peace sign sewn in the center (a large circle with an upside-down, three-legged, letter "Y" in the center). That got a lot of attention. For a motor, it came with a 25 hp outboard set in an engine well. This was a square hole inside the boat that was open to the ocean at the bottom but the sides came high into the boat so the water could not enter. The objective was that an outboard engine could be set in and removed in this hole. When the motor was set fully in the well, the prop was in the water and it could be used to push the boat through the water.

This old boat took on water through the horizontal planks in the teak hull, so I had to pump it out often. If I did not go down to the boat every weekend it took on more water than was safe. So, I decided to put in a battery-driven pump that had a float switch. When the water level reached a certain height, the float would rise with the water and activate a switch to turn it on. When the water was pumped out, the float switch would drop and turn off the pump.

My problem was where to put the discharge hose. I needed more time to locate a place to drill a hole through the hull above the waterline. For now, I simply hung the hose into the engine well. Apparently, unknown to me, the end of the hose reached to the ocean water in the well.

One weekend, I got a call from the marina telling me my boat had sunk and they had called the marine fire department. I put my back out that same morning, so I had not planned to go to the boat that day. But I had no choice and it was painfully difficult to drive to Long Beach where I kept the boat. When I arrived, I was happy to see that the boat had not completely sunk because it did not have any real heavy ballast. Just the top of the cabin was showing above the water. There was already a diver in the water putting a plastic cover over the bottom of the engine well so no water could enter while it was being pumped dry. It did not take too long for them to pump it out and get her floating again.

They asked me why it sank. I had no idea. I knew the boat took on water, but I had put in a bilge pump for that. Then I realized, I had put the bilge pump discharge hose into the engine well and the end must have gone under the water. When the bilge pump, which was located deeper in the bilge below the waterline, turned on and pumped water out, it would then siphon the water back into the boat. This repeated itself until the battery died, then it just siphoned the ocean into the boat. The only real harm done was that the outboard engine was shot, the wallpaper peeled off, and I had to buy a new propane stove.

I never liked the outboard engine because it consumed a lot of gas mixed with oil, so I considered installing some permanent kind of motor like other sailboats. This would be some sort of diesel motor. Unfortunately, there was no way or space for a motor inside the boat that could use a shaft and a prop like other boats. This boat did not even have a bilge like other sailboats. I realized that whatever I did, a prop had to drive the boat via the engine well that was designed for the outboard.

There was only one way this could be done and that was by using hydraulics. I bought a used, large, vertical, single-cylinder diesel motor. It was big and really heavy. It was difficult to find out where to install it. It was too big to put aft where it should go. Anywhere else would interfere with the sleeping or living space, so I decided to put it all the way forward. This was the only place I could put it.

Next, I had to add a hydraulic pump to the engine drive and connect an intake and exit pressure hose to the pump. The exit or pressure hose went to a lever in the cockpit where I could push it forward to go forward, vertical for neutral, and backward for reverse. Then it led to a hydraulic motor and back to the hydraulic pump on the engine. So now I knew what I had to do next and got to work.

I had to figure out a way to drive the boat using the existing well where I used to put the outboard engine. I decided to make it round instead of square by adding curved pieces of wood in the corners. When it was a perfectly round hole, I made a round wooden cylinder that would fit snuggly into this hole and that was also long enough to reach the bottom of the well. The other end would then be above the sides of the engine well so that it could be rotated in any direction and removed when needed.

To the bottom of this cylinder, I attached the motor with the prop. The hydraulic hoses came up through the middle and went to the valve that controlled the direction the prop would turn. From this valve, the hoses were led under the sole or floor, then forward to the pump on the motor.

This cylinder was held in place by putting a 2" x 2" piece of wood across the top of it that extended wider than the cylinder. Then I made a notch on the sides of the well for this cross piece to sit in and prevent it from rotating unless I wanted it to. This rig permitted me to completely remove the cylinder or move it left or right.

It worked perfectly. I could raise the cylinder so the prop would not cause any drag when sailing. If I wanted, I could even steer the boat with this cylinder and make the stern end of the boat go left or right and even do circles in its own length.

There was only one problem. The single-cylinder diesel would cause the boat to bounce up and down slightly with each stroke of the piston. Therefore, I was the only boat in the harbor that put out a 360-degree wake when motoring…but it worked.

After spending a couple of years working on this boat, I had to learn to sail her. Chinese junks have different sails than most other sailboats. There was no track on the un-stayed wooden mast. Instead, the sails were held against the side of the mast with lengths of line with round balls so the sail could be easily raised or lowered.

The sail had many full-length battens (bamboo strips) to hold its shape. There was a rope that led from each batten and joined them together near the bottom to act as the sheet or line that controlled the position of the sail to the wind.

If the boat had too much weather helm (wanted to turn upwind), the sails could be moved forward on the side of the mast to add more sail area forward. The same applied if it had too much lee helm (wanted to fall off the wind or in the same direction as the wind); the sail could be moved more aft (backward).

I had to spend days at the library learning about Chinese Junks and how to adjust their sails and ropes to the battens, etc.

I also learned that the huge rudder had a large, diamond-shaped hole in it that made it easier to move the tiller that controlled the steering. The boat was so different from a traditional sailboat that there were very few people who could help me.

I finally learned how to sail her and with my friend Jerry, we sailed it to Catalina Island twice. The first time we went, we hoped to go along with another boat the same size. It was only about 25 nautical miles to the island so we should have been able to get there in about five hours. We motored out to the pass and then out of Los Angeles harbor and waited for our friend. Hours went by and it was well past noon. We called him on the radio and he said he had difficulty starting his engine and was on his way but the bottom of his boat was so fouled with barnacles that he could only motor at about 2 knots. So, he told us to go on alone.

By now it was after 2:00 p.m. and we had a long way to go. We had no idea what our actual speed was, but it certainly was not fast. We practiced sailing in different directions so we could better understand how to sail a Chinese Junk. The next thing we knew it was getting dark and we had no idea where we were or how far we had to go.

The wind completely died so we started our 25 hp outboard and began motoring as fast as we could. It got dark and fog set in, making it difficult to see anything at all. I saw some kind of light to our left and I wanted to head for it but Jerry told me to continue following my compass direction.

It was nearly midnight when we ran into a mooring ball. We grabbed it and put the line on our cleat and went to bed. We were exhausted. Just after sun-up, a guy in a small powerboat yelled at us to use the stern line as well. We had no idea what he was talking about. Then he explained that there was a line under our boat that is attached to another line that we should attach to our stern so our boat will not swing in a circle banging into other boats.

We had sailed into our destination, the Isthmus Cove. What we did not know was that there was a huge rock in the center of the cove. To enter, you must either pass it on your left or right. We had passed it on our left without even knowing it was there. We both could not believe how lucky we were to sail in that dark fog, not having any idea where we were after changing so many sailing directions and the first thing we hit was a mooring ball. Someone was watching over us on that night.

Later, the next morning we returned to Long Beach without any problem. We made one more trip to the Isthmus after I had installed the hydraulic drive from the diesel engine. That one went well except that the vibration from the single-cylinder diesel kept us kind of bouncing the whole way over and back.

Then I had an offer to buy my old Junk. I realized that if I wanted to do a lot more sailing, this was not the boat, so I sold her.

My Second Boat, Balboa 20: *I name her, "The Trull" "A female who sells herself for money." This is when I gained most of my sailing experience. I could tow this boat behind my van to Mexico or anywhere I wanted to sail. I sailed around the Baja Peninsula in Mexico. This is the true beginning of me living my dream and I gained the confidence to cross oceans.*

I found this 20-foot sailboat that I could put on a trailer and tow behind my van. I couldn't stand up inside of it, but I figured I would spend most of my time outside sailing. Since it was small and made of fiberglass, it did not require much work. I loved the idea that I could take it wherever I wanted to sail it. It only had a tiny 2 hp outboard engine but that was really only needed when entering and leaving the marina because this small boat sailed in almost any conditions. This was my boat for truly learning how to sail.

This Balboa was designed by Lyle Hess, a reputable boat designer who had designed many small, seaworthy sailboats. I had no idea I would meet him one day and we would become close friends.

One of my first experiences on *The Trull* was when Karl, a friend of mine, and I towed it to Oxnard in Southern California. From there we could sail to a group of islands known as the "Channel Islands." These islands had all their anchorages slightly upwind from Oxnard so we knew we would have to sail a bit into the normal winds for this time of year.

As we were launching *The Trull,* a man from the harbor patrol came over and asked us what we were doing. We told him we were sailing out to the Channel Islands. He warned us that a heavy storm was expected that afternoon and we really should not go. For Karl and me this was exactly what we wanted, a heavy weather experience.

We could not point the boat upwind where the anchorage was, so we had to sail a bit to our lee (downwind) side. We eventually passed the south end of the southernmost island and decided to tack or change our direction more upwind. After a few hours, the wind was picking up and we realized we had made no headway at all. So, we put on the little 2 hp outboard and tried to motor to our anchorage. Unfortunately, the winds and waves were increasing. Finally, the outboard got swamped by a wave from the windward side and stopped working. It did not make any difference because it could not push us against the wind.

It was near sunset when we decided to sail back past the south end of the Anacapa or southern island and then try to sail inside the channel between the islands and the mainland. As we rounded the southern point it was dark and all we could see were steep, breaking waves. We were both suddenly aware that we had made a mistake. A wave hit us and knocked us on our side so the sails were in the water. Karl was no longer aboard. I yelled out to him but no answer. The boat would not upright itself because of the suction the sails were creating laying in the water. I let the sheets (ropes that control the sails) loose and the boat suddenly came upright. Then I saw Karl, who had been under the sails. He swam to the boat and quickly got aboard. We dropped all our sails and were again almost knocked down. We decided to just raise the small jib or front sail and sail downwind, away from the crashing waves.

We were now sailing away from the islands and going toward the open sea. We did not have any charts or any other method of determining where we were. All we knew was that the mainland was to our left, but in order to go that way we had to enter the channel again with the huge breaking waves. We tried various methods to keep us sailing dead downwind to open seas, but nothing worked. If we did not have some sail up, we would not be able to steer the boat. All our sails were too big for these winds and seas. We had no idea what to do and were sure we were headed to China.

We both decided that we had to turn to our port (left) and head for the mainland. At least there, if we hit land, we might be able to get off the boat and get to safety. The problem was that our sails were all too big. We decided to raise the forward sail only about halfway and see if we could sail with our beam or port side to the waves.

We tried this and it worked but within an hour we could see the huge waves breaking on top as we approached the channel. Karl was at the helm steering the boat and I was trying to see when a wave was ready to break in the total darkness. All I could see was when the water at the top of the wave turned white. I would yell to Karl to turn to port so our bow would be facing the breaking wave.

This worked for the first two hours then the waves did not seem to be as high or breaking at the top. We took turns steering the boat and keeping watch. To our amazement, we eventually spotted the channel marker lights into the Oxnard channel. We managed to head upwind just enough to make it inside the pass. Immediately, a harbor patrol boat came out to meet us. They had seen us enter the channel and suspected we were in trouble because it was a bad storm. They towed us to their pier where both Karl and I finally felt safe and thankful to be alive. This was an experience that almost changed my mind about crossing oceans. But one thing I knew for sure is that I needed a bigger boat.

After I built up my courage, I started towing *The Trull* to the Sea of Cortez, Mexico during my summer vacations. I did this for three seasons, towing it behind my van to various parts of Baja's Sea of Cortez. Then I decided to sail it from Southern California, all the way around the tip of Baja (Cabo San Lucas) and up the Sea of Cortez to San Felipe where I would trailer it back to California. This meant sailing the entire Baja peninsula on both sides.

This was a great trip. My friend, Jerry Whitworth, went with me on this one and we had some great times as well as some dangerous experiences including several groundings. Since the keel was retractable, it took most of the worry out of it. When sailing in shallower waters, we would simply crank the ballast keel up so we could enter waters only a few feet deep. We could even beach it if necessary or if we wanted to.

Once when we were anchored a little more than a mile or two from La Paz, Jerry suddenly experienced horrible sharp pains in his groin area. He said the pain was unbearable. We needed to get him to a hospital quickly. I considered raising anchor and taking *The Trull* but then we would have to re-anchor before we could go ashore. I figured it was a short distance so it would be quicker in our dinghy that had the 2 hp outboard that would get us there faster. On the way, he lost control of his bladder, and urine was all over the bottom of the boat. Suddenly, the pain was entirely gone. It must have been a kidney stone he had passed. We returned to *The Trull* and sailed to La Paz the next day. The doctor agreed that he must have passed a kidney stone.

The biggest problem we always had was bringing *The Trull* back across the US border. Each time Customs tore the inside of the boat apart and never put anything back where it was. It took us hours to put the boat back together to take it home. Of course, it was because they were looking for drugs.

I learned so much on this boat that I decided I wanted a live-aboard boat that I could sail anywhere in the world. I sold *The Trull* for more than I paid for her but far less than what I had spent to make the necessary changes that were necessary so that I could sail her anywhere I chose.

My Third Boat, Anacapa 40: *I name her the "Marionette," a puppet controlled by strings." A great learning experience about how important it is to have a boat properly surveyed by a reputable surveyor to know if it is worth its value*

I found the Anacapa 40 for sale at a price I could almost afford so I bought her with a small loan from the bank and I lived aboard her in a marina at Dana Point, California. It needed a lot of work to bring it up to my standards. It had a large aft stateroom (bedroom)

with a head (toilet and shower). As you left the aft stateroom you stepped up three steps to the galley (kitchen) that was huge with a dining table. Then you stepped down three steps into the saloon (living room) that was also huge with about 8-feet of headroom. Then just forward was another head and stateroom. The engine was a Perkins 40 hp diesel located under the galley sole (floor).

About a week after I bought her, I was standing looking aft into the stateroom contemplating what I needed to do. As I was standing there, I noticed I had somehow scratched a hole through the bulkhead (wall) where I was standing. The wood on the side of the cabin was all rotten. I contacted the person I had paid to survey the boat for compensation, and he refused.

I went to a maritime lawyer who called the man, and he agreed to pay me $5,000. He said it was all he had. I accepted it and then found a cheap but highly qualified boat carpenter who completely replaced the cabin sides and then fiberglassed over it when he was finished. I then painted her, and she looked great.

I sailed *Marionette* all over Southern California and several times to San Francisco and back. Once we even spent three weeks in the delta of the San Francisco bay area. She was a great sailing boat, fast and stable in rough water.

Now, after sailing her for hundreds of nautical miles, I had gained the experience I felt I needed. I decided that I wanted to go cruising around the world alone, in the *Marionette*.

The problem was that this boat was too big to handle all by myself, so I decided to continue to live aboard her while I began my search to find a smaller, seaworthy boat.

My Fourth Boat, Bristol Channel Cutter 28: *I name her "Xiphias:" from Greek mythology, an underwater sea God that swims on the surface of the water with its dorsal fin exposed like a sail and it has a long spear on the front of its head like a bowsprit." This is the boat I intend to sail around the world. I must build the interior then preparations are made to cross the Pacific*

Early one fine summer morning, the sun showed new and already golden glorious rays intermingled with a gentle breeze that carried with it the smell and taste of the sea. I climbed into my old Pinto station wagon parked at Dana Point Marina. As I headed for Costa Mesa, I had no idea my life was about to change dramatically. I'd been looking for a smaller boat; strong, seaworthy, and not too expensive, and I'd checked out a variety of new and second-hand designs. But they were either too big, too cramped, too costly, too poorly constructed, too ugly, or not strong enough for the ocean cruising I planned to do.

As I merged with traffic, I recalled my conversation a couple of days ago with Lyle Hess, designer of the little 20-footer I'd sailed around Baja, Mexico. Additionally, Lyle had designed Lin and Larry Pardey's 24-foot *Seraffyn*, that they'd sailed around the world and about which they'd written several books. With excitement, Lyle mentioned his latest design, a 28-foot version of *Seraffyn*, one being produced in fiberglass at a yard in Costa Mesa, California. He called this bigger model a Bristol Channel Cutter. His enthusiasm nearly erased the

fact that none of the cutters had yet been put in the water and I heard only Lyle's confidence that she would sail well.

With the sailing experience I'd had, I knew the world was full of beautiful things, places, and people. I wanted to visit them all: Tahiti, Fiji, New Zealand, Australia, Japan, China, Philippines, Melanesia, etc. I longed to eat their foods, live their customs, speak their languages, dive their waters. With something akin to hunger, I craved the adventure of sailing from island to island, continent to continent, hemisphere to hemisphere, anchorage to anchorage. I felt compelled to sail the seas of the world in a yacht of my own.

This obsession had grown over many years. I'd sailed to Baja in *The Trull*, and currently, I lived aboard the *Marionette*. Twice I'd taken her to San Francisco, had sailed to Mexico, and had made many trips to the outer islands off the California coast. But, the *Marionette*, big and comfortable though she was, drained all my finances. As a high school teacher, I wasn't wealthy. Marina fees were high, and the *Marionette* demanded maintenance plus her monthly boat payments. Seven years from now she'd be paid for, but by then she'd need new rigging and sails.

I signaled out of the fast lane and grinned. That could be my metaphor – get out of the fast lane—permanently. But it couldn't be on the *Marionette*. To handle her I required a crew of at least one and finding a good crew wasn't easy. I did not like the way I was living, borrowing money to buy a car, home, boat, etc. I did not see myself spending the major part of my life teaching and fitting into everyday life like everyone else. I had developed a love for sailing after owning several boats over the years. I dreamed I would someday cross oceans. I needed more experience, so I needed someone to sail with me.

Most of my sailing friends had different working schedules than mine. My hippie type, non-working friends were, well, unreliable. Of my single teacher friends, those I enjoyed sailing with had their fill when we were caught in 100-knot winds while anchored behind Santa Barbara Island, off the California coast. Wives of my married teacher friends usually wouldn't let their husbands go for longer than a day sail, and some wives just plain didn't like their husbands sailing.

Sailing with women, in general, had proved disappointing, and it was largely my fault. I liked bright, beautiful ladies who wore hose, high heels, and had long lovely hair. Unfortunately, those types weren't keen on their long hair blowing in a breeze over 10 knots, and they were more interested in suntans than in learning the effects of the slot while sailing to windward.

As I exited the freeway I thought of Joan, a fellow teacher who was my last girlfriend who said she'd like to cruise but only if the boat was roomy and comfortable. Soon after I bought the *Marionette*, Joan moved aboard with me just before the rainy season. After the first rain, we discovered a leak in the teak deck over the hanging closet holding Joan's expensive clothes. The next morning, she left for work in a wet dress spotted with brown water stains.

The following night a new leak brought a continuous stream of water, slightly smaller than the size an infant boy could produce, directly onto our queen-size bed.

Without speaking we rigged, tied, shaped, and wedged various items under the leak and re-directed it into a metal bucket beside the bed. I tried to ignore the shambles we'd created while locating all the paraphernalia needed to accomplish the job. Cranky and irritable, we crawled back into bed. I reached for Joan only to find that the leak had soaked the center of the mattress. However, the stiff way Joan held her body told me she didn't feel like getting close anyway.

The small stream of water flowed constantly into the bucket with the sound of a fire hose. Forty-five minutes later I sat up, put my feet on the cold, soggy, shag carpet, picked up the overflowing bucket, and whispered, "Shit."

"You said it," Joan answered from the far side of the bed, and it was the very far side, for spreading moisture forced us to the respective edges, and eventually into the saloon where we slept on opposite settees.

At 7:30 a.m. it was still raining. With a clenched jaw, Joan departed for work, but when she and I returned home that evening, she smiled, asked about my day; then suddenly stopped when she saw the completely soaked aft stateroom. Luxurious shag carpeting lay underwater at the low point of the floor.

"The mattress isn't too wet," I pointed out as we stared at a piece of plastic I'd used to cover it that morning. But the plastic had prevented the mattress from drying. "I'll just move it into the saloon near the heater. We can sleep on the floor."

Silence.

I removed my shoes, waded to the bed, and yanked. The mattress was so waterlogged that I couldn't budge it. "A drink?" I suggested.

Dispirited, we turned into the saloon, I poured two glasses of chardonnay, but we couldn't sit on the wet settees. The shag carpet squished beneath our feet as we moved to the raised galley, the one dry spot on the boat. Here Joan looked me straight in the eye. "I'm gathering up my sodden, ruined clothes and stuffing them into a plastic garbage bag, then I'm getting into my car and driving back to Newport Beach where I still have a warm, dry apartment waiting for me. Join me if you like. I truly don't give a damn."

So, it appeared I'd probably be sailing solo on an ocean cruise and I needed a craft, I alone, could handle.

I parked at the yard where the Cutter was being built and walked into the office. "Roger Olson," I said, extending my hand to Sam Morse, builder of the 28-footer, "and I'd like as much information as possible on the cutter."

He took a brochure from the top desk drawer and handed it to me, I skimmed the facts: 28' feet on deck, 37 feet overall with her bowsprit, 10-foot beam with full keel, hand-laid solid fiberglass hull, and deck cored with marine plywood. A waterline of 26' 3", draft 4' 10", 14,000-pound unladen displacement ballast with 4,600 pounds of cast lead, carrying nearly 700 square feet of working sail, aluminum mast, stainless steel rigging, and a 13 hp Volvo diesel.

"Come on," Sam interrupted my reading, "You can see one under construction."

I followed him into the yard, and as we entered a huge tin building he said, "We get the hull and deck strength from the many layers of mat and roving that are hand-laid and squeezed smooth after each layer."

We neared the boat hull and the workers wearing masks. "You can have any desired thickness by adding more layers." he continued. "Probably this keel will be about one-and-a-half inches thick and 5/8 to 3/4 inches at the turn of the bilge leaving nearly a 1/2 inch at the top of the hull."

The fiberglass fumes were strong and although I attempted to concentrate, I felt dizzy and nauseous. As I asked, "Can we go outside for some fresh air?" I wondered how the workers managed to do this daily. Even though the building was well-ventilated, the fumes seemed overpowering.

"We can go on to where hull number 32 is being finished," Sam said as I inhaled deeply. "Most of the Cutters are sold unfinished or as boat kits. This helps keep costs down and enables owners to finish them personally." He nodded ahead, "This one, however, was ordered by an Australian doctor who wanted his boat finely finished and fully-equipped."

A guy in jeans was painting the name *Kikorangi* across the transom, and I stopped dead in my tracks. She was beautiful. From the end of the boomkin to the tip of the six-foot bowsprit her lines flowed in a smooth curve. In awe, I stepped closer seeing solid teak decks, taffrail, cockpit combing, bulwarks, wale strake, hatches, and skylight. Not only was all the exterior wood teak, but the entire cabin was trimmed in teak, a hard, brown, waxy wood that holds up well to the elements. The workmanship was the best quality I had ever seen.

The solid bronze portholes gleamed. "Damn," I said, "she sure looks salty. She belongs on the sea. Any idea how she'll sail?"

Sam shrugged. "I honestly don't know. Believe me, I'm as anxious as you to find out because everyone asks the same question. Considering her 26-foot 3-inch waterline and the 673 square feet of sail area, I'd predict she should be quite fast. That long bowsprit with jib and staysail should permit her to point pretty high and..."

Entranced with the cutter, I had stopped listening. I tuned Sam out because quite simply, I was in love. Minutes slipped by before I asked casually, "How much do you figure the *Kikorangi* will cost when completed?"

Probably Sam hoped for the same off-hand manner for he cleared his throat. "Our boats aren't mass-produced. There's no assembly line. We build to our customer's orders exclusively, so we take great care. Truthfully, we can say, 'the yacht's ideal for cruising.' We use the best materials and the highest standard of construction. They're not cheap because it costs more to build this way. We are semi-custom builders and we must use shipwrights to construct these boats. It's not like a boat built with a fiberglass liner that 'snaps' together by a worker off the street." For a second he paused and then added, "These Cutters aren't for everyone."

He'd talked around the price, so I pushed. "Okay, how much for *Kikorangi*, with sails and all? Give me a sail-away number."

He did, and my knees shook. Hell, I could buy a brand new 35-footer for that price and this was only 28 feet. But I couldn't look away from it, she was the most beautiful boat I had ever seen. Here was my cruising boat, but, damn it, one I couldn't afford. Discouraged, I forced myself to thank Sam, assured him he'd hear from me and climbed into my car.

Although my Pinto's interior was warm, I paid little attention. I wanted a boat just like *Kikorangi* and, by God, I'd have one.

As I drove back down the freeway, my mind swam with pictures of the Cutter and how well she was built, while on an inner soundtrack I kept hearing Sam's voice speaking the price. I must have it, I thought, that's it. Of course, I'd felt the same way the first time I saw Bo Derek. Like a mantra I repeated, "I have to have her,"—a Bristol Channel Cutter, that was.

I decided to put the *Marionette* on the market, keeping the price low enough to sell but steep enough to get me out of debt and help buy just the hull and deck of the Cutter. So, I advertised my sloop and hung a hand-painted sign on the bow. But buyers didn't line up.

I went on a crash saving program, placing a large portion of my monthly paycheck into tax-sheltered annuities so I could draw upon them later. I learned to do without, to stay home nights, to eat in and drink less, to spend money only on bare necessities. On weekends I did odd jobs for other boat owners, but still had few inquiries on mine. I sold more personal items and excess gear off the *Marionette* and started making metal sculptures from wax castings as well as gold and silver jewelry. I never claimed to be an artist, but I seemed to be good at it and it brought in extra cruising funds.

Then early on a Saturday morning, while I sat drinking coffee and fantasizing about the cutter, a chubby little bald man walked out on the finger pier. Without asking permission he stepped aboard.

"I'm Robert T. Whitfield and I'm here to buy your boat."

My coffee mug clinked on the cockpit table. "Sure," I almost laughed, "Cash or check?"

He tugged a checkbook from his rear pocket. "For a retainer I'll give you $3,000." From his shirt pocket, he pulled a pen. "How do you spell your name?"

"R-o-g-e-r O-l-s-o-n," I stuttered.

As he wrote I said, "Hey, you're going to give me $3,000 without even knowing my asking price nor how she sails?"

"I'm not concerned about price." Ripping the check from the book he laid it on the table. "We can discuss it during our sail later this morning. I'm meeting some business associates at 10:00, I'll bring them with me. Have plenty of food and some good Scotch aboard. See you at 11:00."

As quickly as Whitfield had appeared, he left. Stunned, I picked up the check. Then, as reality sunk in, I made a quick run to the store, grabbing up bread, cold meat, chips, nuts, and a quart of the best Scotch the convenience mart stocked.

By 11:00 I had sail covers off, sails ready to be raised and the engine warm. Fifteen minutes later Whitfield arrived, dressed in white shorts and a white T-shirt that accentuated his large belly and he wore no shoes.

"My associates couldn't make it, so let's go."

Soon I had the *Marionette* sailing hard to windward, moving beautifully as if she were showing off, and I felt proud of her performance. In rapid succession, Whitfield ate two sandwiches and downed three glasses of straight Scotch.

"The *Marionette's* great in a blow," I said. "In a storm, she heaves to comfortably with the main fully reefed and the storm jib backed."

Through a full mouth, he mumbled, "I don't care about that, I just anchor."

"But what if you're out at sea and the water's too deep?"

"Just drop the anchor into deep water and when I get into shallow water it will grab onto something. It's the land that causes trouble."

Whitfield was full of crap and I shouldn't care if he bought the boat, but I've always had a big mouth so I couldn't leave his statement unchallenged. "You need some storm strategy," I insisted. "Your method would work in a small storm in shallow water, but sometimes it gets rough and you have to go to sea to get away from land or a lee shore."

He smiled and drained the glass. "I'm not going to sail her. She'll serve as my office on Lido Island. I own a real estate business and intend to sell yachts as well as land and houses."

Hurt stabbed that my boat wouldn't be used at sea, but I needed money; I quoted him the price.

Whitfield didn't blink. "I'll have the cash on Monday. I'm buying other boats, too. Could you get me more Scotch, please?"

As I went below for the bottle, his voice trailed behind me down the companionway. "I'm also buying the *Queen Mary*."

With my foot poised on the ladder, I reconsidered. Maybe I better not take the quart topside. I poured a little liquor in his glass; then hid the bottle.

"What are you going to do with her?" I asked when I handed him his drink.

"Gambling ship." He gulped the Scotch. "Outside the country limits, naturally. I'll fly guests out on a helicopter."

Humor him, I thought, as I brought the *Marionette* about and steered toward the marina. To test his knowledge I asked, "How do you plan to get her seaworthy again? I am sure she isn't able to motor out, if her motor works, from where she now sits in Long Beach?"

As he rambled on about engineering experts, I inched the sloop back into her slip. "Mr. Whitfield," I admitted sheepishly, "I could use some cash right now. If you'll give me a hundred dollars, I'll write you a receipt for it and return your check."

Without hesitation, he agreed. "However, the cash is in my hotel room."

Rapidly slipping on my thongs I suggested, "I'll go with you, so you don't have to come back."

"First, we have to find my car, " Whitfield announced as we proceeded along the dock. "I don't remember where I parked it and the hotel keys are in the glove box."

Although quite drunk he walked straight and his description of a white Cadillac convertible, parked near Harpoon Henry's restaurant, was but a bit slurred.

We rounded a corner. A vintage 1959 convertible sat half on the sidewalk and half in the street. Its hood was wired down and stood agape by 6 inches, had no trunk lid, a cracked windshield without wipers, a missing interior panel, and upholstery that had experienced the butts of thousands. How had this car managed to stay on the road?

Whitfield was delighted. "Oh, here it is." And as he rummaged through the glove box, minus a door, I felt despair. Maybe he's an eccentric I assured myself. Maybe he's – and for a second, I imagined the *Kikorangi*. As long as there was a chance this man would make my dream possible, I'd stick with him.

When he couldn't find the hotel or car keys, I accompanied him the short distance to the Dana Point Hotel. Here the elderly female clerk behind the desk addressed him by name. I felt hopeful, but she quickly added, "The police were here asking for you, but I told them they couldn't search your room without a warrant. What's…"

"Damn." He beat his fists against the countertop. "They do this to me whenever I'm handling a big business deal. Well, just give me the spare set of keys."

She shook her head. "Remember you lost your first set of keys this morning and I gave you the spare. All I have left are the master keys and I can't give you those."

Whitfield leaned his big belly against the edge of the counter and bent far over so his nose nearly clipped the clerk's forehead. In a voice of quiet authority – one that again raised my hopes – he said. "I have come to your hotel on business, big business. I have a client with me. I don't care about your keys. I'll buy this damn place and put you out in the street if you don't let me use that set instantly."

She was intimidated thoroughly, so she immediately handed over the keys. Whitfield punched the elevator button and we rode to the second floor. His room commanded a great view of the marina and, once more, I was unsure of him. He fumbled for his checkbook.

"No check. Cash."

As if awakening from a dream he said, "Well, why didn't you say so? My cash is hidden in the car."

Hope had fled. I wanted to get away and eagerly left with him. But when the elevator door opened on the lobby level he blanched at the policemen. They faced the counter, so Whitfield gripped my arm, jerked me to one side and we hurried out a rear door whispering something about finding his secretary by the pool.

He started on some wild story about a metal plate in his head during the war and asked me to feel it, but I didn't. He continued talking about becoming deranged when he spotted a man in any uniform, but I yelled, "Hey, Whitfield, or whatever your name is, you're so full of bullshit you can't see for the brown in your eyes. You haven't any money, and if your check bounces, I'm going to prosecute."

With considerable dignity, he drew himself up. "I can't blame you for what you must think. In your shoes, I'd feel the same way. Take my check to the bank on Monday. I'll be back next weekend. You can apologize then."

Continuing to hold himself erect, and mustering as much dignity as any man can with half a quart of Scotch in his belly, he strolled back toward the hotel. Once more weak hope nudged. Could he be legit? But, suddenly, just before the door he turned into the shadows and was gone from sight.

His check bounced, but I saved it as a souvenir of the day I met the guy who was going to buy the *Queen Mary*. The check reminded me of what I'd learned about selling a boat and of what I would go through for the cutter.

Amazingly, a few weeks later a genuine buyer accepted my asking price. I paid off what I owed and with the remaining money went to Costa Mesa. For most of an afternoon Sam and I discussed prices and specifications, so that by the time I left his office I'd ordered a Bristol Channel Cutter with hull and deck assembled, lead ballast, structural bulkheads, and some internal woodwork completed. Out of money, I'd wait before ordering anything else.

Broke or not, I drove away from that boatyard euphoric. My dream was becoming a reality, I felt invincible. Traffic didn't bother me. I smiled when someone cut me off. Life was wonderful. Now that I had sold my boat, I needed a place to live. Even this proved magical. When I checked the newspaper ads for rooms to rent, I circled several possibilities in the Costa Mesa/Newport Beach area where I preferred to stay because that's where my boat would be built.

I pulled up before a house in Newport Beach and a young landlady invited me in. As she explained the rental agreement details, I didn't listen carefully. Instead, I studied her short blonde hair, pretty blue eyes, and cute petite figure. But then, a beautiful, long-haired brunette joined us in the living room. She smiled, sat on the couch, crossed her long shapely legs, and said she was the other tenant. From then on, I heard nothing, for she was quite buxom. She could smuggle melons. I wondered how she could ever sleep on her stomach. Well, I thought if I'm lucky, I'll learn.

"There is another tenant," I heard the landlady say. Another woman?

"He's away most of the time, so usually there would be just the three of us."

I was afraid that someone else might get the room, so I paid the first and last month's rent and moved in that night.

In an effort not to appear too eager around these unmarried ladies, I tried to act cool. But my stomach knotted and every hormonal gland over-reacted.

On weekday mornings I drove off to school and about 4:00 p.m. visited the boatyard to observe the painfully slow building process. Indeed, it took two months before the deck could be fastened to the hull, and at the end of that time, she was still far from ready. Daily I reminded myself of Sam's warning, "It takes time to build a boat right."

After checking on the Cutter's progress I hurried to the house, showered, blow-dried my hair, and ruffled it a bit to make it seem I'd done nothing to it. I dabbed on a trace of cologne, carefully picked what to wear, and sauntered into the living room.

The weeks passed, unfortunately, neither woman showed any physical interest in me. All either of them seemed to admire was my cooking. But, when the big-breasted brunette smiled, "I just love your spaghetti," I wasn't sure if she really did or if my cooking simply permitted her to leave the house earlier.

And, unfortunately, I quickly learned that both lovelies had special boyfriends. I met them, and all the other special men that the others weren't supposed to know about.

One night while I lay imagining what was going on behind the closed bedroom doors, I recognized I hadn't a chance with the blonde or the brunette. I faced great competition and living in such proximity to them was more of a hindrance than a catalyst. Also, I recognized that the environment wasn't doing my hormones any good.

I hit the singles bars—a mistake. Sure, contact there eased my hormonal problem but I never met anyone with whom I cared to start a relationship. Occasionally Joan and I had a drink. After the experience on the *Marionette*, Joan and I had continued to see each other. Although she refused to move back aboard after I repaired the boat, we were good together. She and I shared many similar interests and communicated well. Because of this communication, we came to the same conclusion. We were much better friends than lovers.

But the salvation, of course, the true woman I needed was my boat. Sam agreed that I could work on it during weekends. I wanted her as complete as possible before she went into the water because on that day, regardless of her condition, I intended to move aboard.

During this period of limbo, I made one of the most important decisions of my life. I set a date to depart on my cruise—just over a year away, the first day after school was dismissed. As if that decision altered time, days passed more rapidly. Every afternoon and every Saturday and Sunday I visited the boat. In the evenings I jogged about five miles before studying Morse code for an amateur radio license. After tapping out dots and dashes, I prepared halyards, sheets, and anchor lines.

As days neared the launch date, I doubled efforts to find a name for the boat, something unusual, something that would suit her character. Friends suggested *The Jolly Roger, Free Spirit,* and *Roger's Dream.*

With an arched eyebrow, Joan said, "What about *Nemesis?*"

I grinned. "Don't you think *Wet Dream* might be more appropriate?"

At the library as I thumbed through various books, I came across a picture of a fish god or monster:

Xiphias; originating from Greek mythology, an undersea fish God that swims on the surface of the water with its dorsal fin exposed (*like a sail*). It has huge sharp teeth and a long spear on its head (*like the bowsprit on a sailboat*). It is the fastest thing in the water (*under the sun... until... man was done*).

"*Xiphias,*" I tasted the word. It sounded right. It fit the boat with its long bowsprit.

Triumphant, I informed friends but when their version came out close to "syphilis," I said, "The X sounds like a Z. It's pronounced Zifias."

I hired a sign-writer to paint the name on the stern, but that meant I needed to add a home port. I called the Coast Guard station, explained that my boat wasn't yet afloat, that I intended to document her, and wondered what hailing port I must use.

"You have three choices," the officer said. "The city where the coast guard station is located…"

Los Angeles, I thought.

"Or the place where you reside…"

Soon I'd be living on *Xiphias*, but friends in San Juan Capistrano said I could use their address.

"Or the place where the boat was built."

Bingo. I chose Costa Mesa, California.

Next, I debated whether to have an engine. I listed the advantages and disadvantages. The major negatives: cost, weight, difficulty, expense of repair, the possibility of leaking thru-hulls, and the amount of room consumed. On the positive side: I could use electrical direct current lighting because an engine would keep the batteries charged; it could provide power through narrow channels and in calm conditions, it could save me in a dangerous situation and would allow me to take the boat places I couldn't get to without power. Advantages won, and I opted to install an engine along with a small diesel tank.

That meant adding two more through the hull skin fittings, water intake, and an exhaust. I hated drilling any more holes in the hull than were necessary because thru-hull fittings are always a possible cause of a sinking. Fittings can break off or hose clamps can rust or break so the hose comes loose releasing water inside the boat. Since fittings are usually below the waterline, they can siphon the ocean into the boat. So, I'd have no more than three below the water line: the engine intake, the cockpit drain, and the sink drain.

Yet, what about a toilet? That would require two additional hull fittings, one as the water intake, one as the discharge. As I considered. I rubbed my forehead, remembering the night on the *Marionette* when I'd awakened to find saltwater flowing over the toilet rim, filling the bilge. My heart raced as I remembered how I'd found the anti-siphon hole plugged, how the one-way valve was working both ways, and how I realized that had I not been aboard, she would have sunk right there in the harbor.

Then there was the afternoon I sailed the *Marionette*, plowing to windward. One of my crew went below to use the forward head. "Roger," he'd yelled, "she's filling with water."

In that case, water had been forced back up through the exhaust from the hydraulic effect of the boat's acceleration. Once more, the one-way valve had worked both ways.

I thought back to my first boat, *Peace of Junk*, that had sunk in its slip at the Long Beach Marina, because a bilge pump hose siphoned the ocean back aboard.

The parade of memories settled it. I would build a cedar bucket to use like in the olden days. A close friend volunteered to build it for me as a parting gift. When it was finished it was beautiful with a cedar seat and lid. I couldn't use it. It looked too good. Therefore, I varnished the exterior, fiberglassed the interior, and stuck a plastic bucket inside. The inserted bucket could be removed, carried outside, and its contents heaved overboard. I admit it sounds a bit barbaric and crude. However, after I'd been cruising awhile, I learned that most sailors do close off their boat heads during passage and rely on buckets.

On launching day, I awoke before dawn. I don't think I slept much during that hellishly long night, for hundreds of problems had danced through my mind. Because *Xiphias* had to be moved about five miles on a truck from the yard to the launch site, I imagined the hull slipping. Powerless to stop her, I saw her crash onto the concrete and heard her shatter. I blinked, but the next sequence showed a crazed driver smashing into the transport truck. I even created an earthquake. "Be calm," I whispered aloud, "she'll get there safely."

But, then, some inner devil prodded, "She'll be lifted from the cradle, which has supported her from the beginning, and she'll be suspended, no, dangled, in the air by only two nylon slings."

"Shut up! She will be, she just has to be, set gently into the water."

My future is dependent on this boat. It is my one-way ticket out of this hectic, materialistic rat race. It will take me to new cultures and beautiful tropical islands. My new life is ahead of me and this boat is the means. Every penny I own is in this dream, I can't lose it now.

Unable to eat breakfast I left for the yard. As the transport truck driver attempted to jack *Xiphias* up so he could get his trailer beneath the cradle, it rocked from side to side and I paced back and forth, bit my fingernails, kicked posts, bricks and dirt.

"Come on," Sam said and firmly grasped my arm. He opened the passenger door of my car and pushed me in. "Hey," he called to my friend Bob who had just arrived to help, "Take this guy away before he has a heart attack."

Bob drove me to the launch site, but it wasn't any better there. Like an expectant father who can't stand to be in the delivery room and yet can't stand not being there more. I felt divided. So, again, I bit nails, threw stones, and kicked cans, paper, anything.

"Here she comes," Bob said as the truck eased close to the shore. While I held my breath *Xiphias* was quickly lifted onto slings and suspended over the water.

In a voice that shook I said to Sam's wife, Betty, "Will you do the honors?"

She clutched the expensive champagne bottle by the neck with her right hand and in a stronger voice than mine announced, "I christen thee, yacht *Xiphias* of Costa Mesa." With a tennis backhand, she flung the bottle against the bow stem. The damn bottle didn't break! Over and over she struck the bow. Gel coat flew everywhere, but the bottle remained intact.

"Hit the stainless-steel bobstay," Sam said, so with another swing and another aim, Betty connected. Glass and champagne burst into the air, and *Xiphias* was set afloat.

For good luck, I placed a silver dollar beneath the mast before it was stepped. Tradition calls for a gold coin, but I reasoned that wise Neptune would understand the price of gold and would settle for silver.

After setting the mast, adjusting the rigging, running the engine, and finding that everything worked, I and those involved with building

the boat, jumped on board to set off on our first sail. We raised the main, then the staysail, and finally the jib. New white sails bellowed out with the wind and as *Xiphias* pulled away from the dock, gathering speed, I felt acceleration, a new sense of power. This baby was fast!

I could hardly wait to live aboard. Gone were thoughts of the blonde landlady and the buxom brunette. Gone were memories of all I'd undergone to be here today. All that was important was that *Xiphias* was pointing into the wind, better than I'd expected. She was fast, stiff, comfortable, and beautiful. We sailed in-and-out, up-and-down, zig-zagged through moored boats. People working on boats or lounging on decks stared as we scooted past. I sensed *Xiphias'* pride and I could almost detect a touch of arrogance as she sailed by a fast-moving 36-foot ketch.

Too soon, we returned to the dock and unloaded everyone except for a few who asked to help sail her to her berth at Dana Point.

Now, time accelerated even more. I left my female housemates and moved aboard where I began building an interior around my clothes and sleeping bag. I followed a repetitive schedule.

After teaching, I ran four miles and then worked on *Xiphias* until exhausted, then I showered, and slept. Yet life was full and I was happy. I would sail *Xiphias* and begin my dream of world cruising, and it would be soon.

Chapter 3
Two Lovers Meet

The bright cabin light revealed Cindy's deep green eyes and freckles scattered across her nose. She was more desirable in the light than in the darkness.

One evening, soon after launching *Xiphias*, I took my standard late afternoon run. As I headed back toward the gate leading down to the boat, a little, dark-haired girl darted in front of me, and though I swerved, I still brushed against her.

"You okay?" I gasped.

"My mum runs, too, but she doesn't knock over children."

Then she grinned and I realized she was joking.

Panting, I asked, "How 'bout you? You jog with her?"

"No, she's too fast for me, but I can run almost as fast."

Out of the corner of my eye, I could see, hand in hand, an adult dark-haired female and a very small blonde girl, advancing.

"Does your father run, too?" I asked just as the mother stepped before the girl, obviously protecting her from this strange, puffing sex villain.

Directing my attention to the woman I said, "I'm Roger. Your daughter and I were just discussing running. She says you are a runner, too."

"Yes," she answered coldly, "When I have the time."

She had the voice of an angel, the face of a movie star, and the personality of a polar bear. As she and the children turned away, I said, "Hey, don't leave. I'd like to chat, just as soon as I catch my breath."

She hesitated, then leaned on the handrail, and gazed out over the marina. The small blonde girl ran down the walkway with the taller girl chasing after her. I rested against the rail beside this queen, but not too close, should my sweaty body offend her.

"I introduced myself as Roger. Should I just call you 'Mum'?"

She continued to study the boats, magically yellowed from the light of a slowly rising full moon. Either she hadn't heard me or was ignoring me, I thought, but at last, she spoke, "Sorry I'm Cindy."

"You have lovely girls," I said, hoping to maintain the conversation.

She regarded the kids, now behind us, and for the first time, smiled. "Ashley's eight and Chris is almost two." I couldn't help staring at her. She had to be about 25, was gorgeous, and smelled like exotic talcum powder. She couldn't be any taller than 5' 3" and definitely was petite. I couldn't see her figure because she wore a long, patterned, very feminine dress like my grandmother used to wear. Her shiny, nearly straight black hair reached down below her shoulders. I couldn't tell the color of her eyes, but they looked like laughing eyes, round on top and flat on the bottom. Her nose was perfect. I longed to grab her, hold her close, feel her warmth, smell her hair, and kiss her mouth. Instead, I asked, "You live at Dana Point?"

She stared directly into my eyes and my knees began to wobble. "No, in Corona Del Mar. We had dinner here at the Mexican restaurant." Her husband must be a lawyer or doctor because that is one wealthy town.

After a pause, she asked, "And, you? Do you usually run at the marina? Live close by?"

Maybe I'd caught her interest, so I relaxed a bit and gestured to the right. "Yes, I live on a boat just down the gangway. I start my run at this gate and end…"

"I love boats." Her face lit up. "I come to the marina often just to look at them. Someday I'll own a yacht and I'll sail the seas of the world."

Unbelievable. A beautiful woman…a yacht…sail the seas!

"Would you like to see my boat?" And as I spoke, I realized I sounded pretty awkward. "I'm working on her, but at least she's presentable, just a few tools lying around."

With the kids, we walked to where *Xiphias* lay snugly in her slip. In the moonlight, she seemed alive. Her varnish sparkled, she looked "salty," and I felt proud of her, but when we went below I was stunned. With the bare wood and lumber scattered about, the interior looked chaotic. I tossed aside wood and tools, clearing a space for Cindy and Ashley to sit. With wide eyes, Chris surveyed the cabin, then grasped my hand and said, "Boat." Everyone laughed and I nodded, "Yep, Chris, it is a boat."

The bright cabin light revealed Cindy's deep green eyes and freckles scattered across her nose.

We talked for hours. Ashley asked many questions and Chris played "Captain Hook," walking the plank and threatening us with her one-foot ruler sword she picked up off the plywood seat. At about 10:30, Cindy jumped up. "I've got to get the kids home. It's way past their bedtime."

This was my final opportunity to discover her marital status. "Hope your husband won't be upset that you kept the children out so late."

Her laughing eyes glistened, and her smile broadened, but before she could speak, Ashley said, "Daddy and mummy are divorced, so you can come to visit us anytime you want. You and mummy could run together on the beach and you could take us sailing."

"Ashley, you little twerp," Cindy said. "Don't be so forward."

Atta, girl, Ashley, I thought. I like your style; a big mouth just like me.

Blushing, Cindy patted Ashley on the head, "This little monster's trying to fix me up, I think."

But I reached over and touched the girl on the shoulder. "You're on my side. I'd love to visit your home, and I promise we'll sail in about two weeks if your mum comes, too."

Then I looked at Cindy, our eyes met, and it became noticeably quiet. We held each other's gaze and simultaneously smiled. I penciled Cindy's phone number onto a piece of wood before walking them to their car.

As they drove off, I suddenly thought how nice it could be to be a family man, to have those two girls as my own. Something I'd never before considered. I wanted to call her as soon as I got back on *Xiphias*, but decided I'd better not appear as eager as I felt.

In the middle of the week, I phoned Cindy inviting her to dinner, and when she agreed, I felt the whole world belonged just to me. Each day that passed before our date made me nervous, and I ran hard trying to dispel my anxiety.

On the day of our date, my stomach knotted, my hands trembled. Nothing must go wrong. I polished my shoes, but not too much for I didn't want her to think I was too neat. I selected my least wrinkled shirt and pants, dusted off the sawdust, and in a sweaty palm I clutched the directions she'd given for her address.

It was a cute white house, only a short distance from the beach, and Ashley opened the door, explaining in her grown-up manner that mom was at the store. Taking my hand, she gave me a tour. My first sight, a gray Shepherd. He growled, his fangs gleamed, and he crouched as if to rip out my throat. Right then I resolved to give up my life but was unsure whether to run or turn my back.

Ashley stepped before me and patted the large animal, who instantly became a slobbering puppy. "Mugs" won't bite but beware of her tongue." Ashley was right. Mugs, a big lover, sniffed my hand, licked it, and stayed next to me for the rest of the time I was in the house.

On Ashley's tour, she pointed out what she and her mum had built, painted, and decorated. Chris played with dolls in her room, but she dashed over, reached for me, and said, "Boat." Thus, the three of us, plus Mugs—who sat on the floor with her head in my lap, drooling on my slacks—were on the living room sofa when Cindy entered. "Now," she laughed, "that's making yourself at home. The only things missing are a pipe and slippers."

After the babysitter showed up, I took Cindy to a vegetarian restaurant. I had no idea what she liked, but this restaurant's food would convert the heartiest meat-eater. Plants and flowers filled the restaurant, a female flutist played contemporary jazz, and Cindy and I sank into a dark cubicle surrounded by soft music, soft fragrances. In such an atmosphere, we talked easily about everything.

I talked about my parents who lived in Fresno, how they'd raised me with love and affection. I bragged about Ron, my big brother-protector, who was married with five children.

"I have a mother and father, but they are separated, a younger sister and a brother," Cindy said.

I reminisced about my best friend Jerry Whitworth who lived with his wife in San Francisco. "I met him in the Navy, now he is a career man."

"Figures, " she said.

I frowned.

"Boats."

"Yeh, Jerry sailed with me from San Diego, around Baja, Mexico, and back to San Felipe, Mexico, in a 20-foot trailerable boat."

Cindy leaned forward. "How far?"

"About 2,500 nautical miles. It took us two months to sail around Baja. We spent weeks at some anchorages, overnight at others. We met warm, welcoming Mexicans, shared their hospitality and conversation."

She seemed to hang on every word.

"Of course we suffered from mosquito bites, sunburn, and storms. We dragged anchors and banged into submerged rocks. It wasn't easy and it sure as hell wasn't comfortable, but it was cruising and I loved it."

I stared at her. God, she was lovely. I could just barely pick up that talcum smell and I felt weak. I wanted to quit talking and just watch her, but when she asked about cruising, I went on. "Not only do I love it but I am considering taking a year off from teaching to go cruising. I'm burned out with teaching." I admitted that I liked the barrio school and that I was good at teaching metalworking, drafting, and math. However, I was also frustrated with the administration, and with the new restrictions requiring me to spend most of my time forcing students to tuck in their shirts, or sending them to the office because their hair was too long.

As a school psychologist, Cindy agreed. So we exchanged teaching ideas and compared notes on students, but we always reverted to the subject of boats.

After dinner, we drove to the beach where the moon rose full and high in the sky. It carved yellow-orange, snake-like reflections across the rolling swells as they approached land. Removing our shoes, we wandered hand in hand down the beach, wondering about the sea and its magnetism. Cindy stopped and faced the horizon. "Someday I want to visit all those tropical islands out there, eat coconuts, and lay in the sun " I stepped behind her, wrapped my arms around her tenderly, and let the heat from her body caress my skin.

"Something tells me you're going to have your dream come true sooner than you think," I whispered as I kissed the top of her head.

As often as possible we saw each other again and again. Our love deepening with each meeting. Time apart was spent anticipating being together. I couldn't remember when I'd been as happy as I was during those days of getting to know Cindy.

I worked hard on the boat and in a couple of weeks, *Xiphias* was complete enough for me to take Cindy and the girls out for day sails. While Chris was a natural sailor, Ashley tended to get seasick, but she never complained. The first we knew of her distress was when she told Cindy, "mum, my stomach's coming up."

Cindy, as at home on the sea as she was on land, wanted to sail farther. "Let's not take the girls next time," she suggested. "That way I can concentrate on learning to sail."

And by unspoken agreement, we knew we could also concentrate on each other. It would be our first chance to be alone together since meeting over two months ago.

"Okay, what about Santa Cruz Island, off the Santa Barbara coast? It's a good sail and can be challenging at times." I said, thinking back to my fiasco with Karl on the 20-foot Balboa.

"This time will be different," Cindy promised, and it was. I spent the five most idyllic days I could recall, finding the 90-mile upwind sail an adventure, capped by the novelty of having Santa Cruz island exclusively to ourselves. We explored anchorages, swam, read, hiked, listened to music, practiced sailing techniques, and made love and more love.

This was our first real sea test for *Xiphias*. She sprang to life as soon as we stowed the anchor and winched sails tight. She acted like a horse who'd been locked in a barn too long and yearned for pasture. She was strong and fast. She felt comfortable and solid sailing through the water instead of over it like so many light boats do. She displayed a developing personality. While she responded to sailing with the wind from any direction, she didn't want me on her bowsprit changing sails while she pushed through seas and headwinds. Politely, but firmly, she dunked me to my neck a few times. I got the message.

She preferred sailing to windward when she needn't carry so much sail area on the main. When feeling overburdened by the wind, she merely dipped her side underwater to soak my seat.

But, when Cindy took the helm, *Xiphias* shone. She never dunked Cindy, granted her every request, and made me feel like a merman being reeled in by two women.

On our return journey to Dana Point, Cindy and I planned future weekend sailing trips with the girls. And, thus, on those expeditions, we'd learn that Chris, who couldn't even see over the cabin, especially enjoyed steering and shouting orders as she held the tiller. And that Ashley, old enough to get bored, needed something to do, so I taught her to tie knots. Swiftly she mastered the basic ones and graduated to the fancy kind, like the "Turks head." Ashley became the ship's steward. When things got a bit rough, she took Chris below, closed ports, and checked that everything was secure and watertight.

Although *Xiphias* seemed small with all of us aboard, we were so happy that no one cared. Happy; that term summed up this period of my life.

After school each afternoon I worked on the boat, then drove to Cindy's where we, plus Mugs, went to the beach for a run. Mugs ran close to my side until having had enough she trotted back to where Chris and Ashley played in the sand.

When we returned to the house, Cindy fixed dinner, Ashley did homework, Chris played with her dolls, and Mugs never gave up trying to fit her oversize body into my lap.

Nightly, Chris demanded that "Boat" kiss her, and Ashley expected a hug. "After all," she'd remind her mother, "I'm the one who found Roger, so I deserve the right to have my own kiss and hug."

After the girls were in bed, Cindy and I sprawled on the living room floor, listening to mild jazz. One evening, while classical music floated over us like an ephemeral blanket, she said carefully, "I've been doing a lot of thinking, why don't I sail with you on your first passage? The girls can stay with my mother."

Speechless, I kissed her, then said, "I wish *Xiphias* were big enough to take the whole family." Yet, we knew that we should experience weeks at sea to determine if we should expose children to the hardships of ocean passages on such a small yacht.

"Okay," she grinned, "all settled. Now, we have to prepare for the cruise."

Chapter 4
The Preparation

We went below and, suddenly, the realization that we'd soon be living our dream intoxicated us. As we stood in the aisle, Cindy clasped my hand. "We're going to have a wonderful passage with light seas and fair winds. I know it."

Our departure date was just over a month away, but where to go? Hawaii and then on to Tahiti? Sail along the Mexican coast and eventually cut across to the Marquesas? Or head directly for the Marquesas?

I borrowed government pilot charts which Cindy and I studied along with sailing directions during June. We pondered the advantages and the disadvantages of each possibility, but our main problem was time, for Cindy had but a little over two months of summer vacation. Considering her schedule, we opted to sail straight for the Marquesas, about 3,200 nautical miles.

Early one Saturday morning we drove to San Pedro to buy necessary charts and navigational publications. I stuffed my wallet with new, crisp 20-dollar bills, more than enough to purchase everything needed, or so I believed. Surprise number one: multitudes of charts; those of the passage to and between islands and individually detailed charts of significant bays and anchorages. Surprise number two: cost. No way could I afford all the charts I wanted, so I settled for important ones of the Marquesas, the Tuamotus, and Tahiti. Additionally, I selected Pilot Charts for the South Pacific and these government publications: Worldwide Marine Weather Broadcasts, the Admiralty List of Lights and Fog Signals, Radio Navigational Aids, and Sailing Directions for the South Pacific Islands, Vol I and II. Most of these were of little use I discovered later.

We left San Pedro with an empty tank of gas and a wallet so thin that I could only pump three dollars' worth of fuel into the car.

Xiphias was completed, well, complete enough for us to depart in June. I longed to buy many items, such as a canvas dodger to cover the companionway when it got wet, but the dodger would spoil the boat's lovely lines so I placed a higher priority on a wind vane to steer the boat. I hate to think what it would be like hand steering any boat across an ocean. The wind vane steers the boat at a set angle to the wind. If the wind direction changes, so does the course of the boat. Commercially available units proved disappointing. They were ugly or looked like an oil derrick set on the back of the boat. Some were unreliable, others were too bulky, some were not as efficient on an outboard rudder and all were exorbitantly priced.

Lin and Larry Pardey, who had nearly completed their circumnavigation on *Seraffyn*, returned to Newport Beach and sailed with us one weekend. Larry described the steering mechanism he'd designed for *Seraffyn*, just a trim tab connected to the outboard rudder.

I made a few modifications but stuck to the basic principle Larry had described and to my surprise, the mechanism held *Xiphias* on course in any wind. Since our new mechanical crew person would stand many more watches than Cindy or me, it deserved a name.

I had read something about a sail used for steering on old clipper ships, so I checked out the library book I'd skimmed while searching for my boat's name. I learned that the aft sail, called a Spanker, was attached to the mizzen mast and it helped balance the helm. Thus, our vane became "Spanky."

Next, we considered a life raft. "We could cruise for almost a year on the cost of one life raft," I said. "*Xiphias* is so small, where could we secure it on deck?" Cindy asked, "and since rafts must be inspected regularly by a reputable company, how is that possible while cruising?"

Thus, we began our rationalizing about the life raft. We asked ourselves under what conditions we'd resort to one. In case of a monumental storm, one that *Xiphias* couldn't survive, the raft certainly wouldn't survive either. If we hit a reef, we'd stay afloat and probably sit on the reef indefinitely or at least long enough to use a hard dinghy or an inflatable one. If a floating object, such as a container from a ship or a massive log, or even a whale holed *Xiphias*, it would be best to have a life raft. On the other hand, if the hole wasn't too big and was accessible, I could temporarily plug or seal it, and if time permitted could dive overboard and stuff a sail into or around the hole.

Weighing the odds, we said, "No," to the life raft. Our friends and family were appalled. Chided for our casual attitude, bombarded with clichés like "when you need one cost won't matter," we also received books and magazine articles. *Survive the Savage Sea*, *Bailey's Staying Alive*, *Survival at Sea*, and *Attacked by Killer Whales*, mysteriously appeared at school, in my mailbox, and in our cockpit.

Cindy and I capitulated with a compromise. Our existing "Metzler" inflatable would serve double duty, as an inflatable dinghy and as an emergency life raft. Of primary importance is inflating a raft quickly, so we had to figure how to inflate the dinghy without damaging the rubber or subjecting it to too much pressure. Carbon dioxide (CO_2), the logical choice, was so cold when discharged it could freeze and crack the rubberized skin.

Friends recommended helium, oxygen, freon, and some other unlikely gases, but we chose compressed air—safe and readily available. After purchasing a small, empty CO_2 fire extinguisher I fit it with a standard "J" valve from an old scuba tank. To this valve, I fastened a standard scuba regulator fitting. Instead of a regulator, we fashioned two hoses and a "Y" valve. From the tank fitting, each hose led to a separate chamber on either side of the Metzler. We vulcanized new connections to the top chambers so the hoses could connect without blowing loose during inflation.

It required some experimentation to determine the exact amount of air needed to fill both chambers and the correct number of P.S.I.s. Additionally, we learned that when the compressed air was released, the chambers filled in under 45 seconds. Lastly, we attached the tank to the wooden transom with stainless steel hose clamps.

We put the inflatable on the garage floor and crawled inside. In an emergency, we'd need to pump up the inflatable floor but that would present no important problem. The important problem was trying to visualize being thrown around in an angry sea. We laid on the bottom waiting for the sun and then imagined intense rays cooking us to medium-rare.

With Cindy's head against my shoulder, I murmured, "There's only one way to beat killer heat, take off your clothes."

"That will only make it hotter. We need some kind of canopy to cover and protect us from the elements." Her elbow jabbed my side, "and from children looking out their bedroom windows."

The Metzler had rubber eyes vulcanized to the top of the chambers for sail attachment, so by sliding 3/4-inch PVC tubing through these eyes and then fitting various elbows to form the joints, we constructed a canopy frame. Completely detachable, it could be stowed in a nylon bag wrapped up in the dinghy. No piece of tubing measured more than 20 inches and we numbered each piece in waterproof ink to ensure quick and easy assembling.

Cindy sewed a canopy out of ripstop nylon in "distress orange." It took many hours of fitting and cutting before the canopy fit tightly over the frame. She sewed numerous nylon ties to the canopy to hold it in place and to reinforce the frame. A drawstring in the hem helped seal the connection between canopy and raft. We left the back of the raft open so we could get in or out, fish, or look for rescue ships.

To protect this aft open section, Cindy sewed Velcro tape onto the canopy and vulcanized it onto the aft part of the raft's chambers. Now the canopy could be sealed tightly to the stern, allowing us to peel back either or both sides of the stern flaps for ventilation or to adjust for shade. If desired, we could roll up the whole section and tie it out of the way.

After countless hours of debate about emergency provisions for our homemade life raft, we whittled our list to:

EQUIPMENT

- Emergency radio beacon and Detachable Harpoon and extra batteries (EPIRB)
- Fishing Gear
- First Aid Kit
- Muslin for sifting plankton
- Flashlight and Batteries
- Cigarette Lighter
- Can Opener

- *Solar Still, for making water*
- *Sea Soap*
- *Radar Reflector*
- *Signal Flare Gun*
- *Solar Blanket*
- *Extra Flares*
- *Knife and Sharpener*
- *Compass*

FOOD

- *Wheat Germ Oil*
- *Granola*
- *Instant Gatorade*
- *Four Packets Beef Jerky*
- *Hard Lemon Candy*
- *Three Packets of Gum*
- *Four Cans of 'C' Rations, Army Surplus*
- *A Pure Protein*

- *Sun cream Ointment*
- *Note Pad and Pencils*
- *Sea Anchor*
- *Needle and Thread*
- *Raft Repair Kit*
- *Signal Mirror*
- *Sponge*
- *Reading Books*

- *Two Packets of Pilot Biscuits*
- *Trail mix*
- *Canned Meats*
- *Various Vitamins*
- *Canned Cheese*
- *Dried Fruit*
- *Unsalted Nuts*
- *Six Cans of Fruit Nectar*

At a construction site, we found two five-gallon discarded paint buckets, perfect to hold emergency items. The buckets were fastened to the raft by a clip at the end of a long line and could float on the water's surface because of air trapped inside.

To solve the water problem, we elected to carry an extra 15 gallons in a bright yellow container tied on deck. In an emergency, we could cut it loose and it would float if we left an air pocket on top. To the handle, we fastened a bright red buoy so we could easily sight it.

Satisfied with the life raft, we wondered where to store all the gear. The raft must be rolled up with the air tank and wooden transom connected making a rather bulky package. It would fit into the lazarette compartment at the back of the boat, but getting it out in an emergency could prove difficult. With no room on deck, we decided to store the raft and its gear in the cockpit. Now the cockpit looked like a junkyard.

"Well, the tiller is always removed while underway because Spanky's going to be steering," Cindy said, "so we can then lounge with our legs stretched out into the cockpit area. If we completely cover the cockpit it would provide even more lounging space. We could even sleep outside."

"But, by covering it we can't get at the engine controls," I replied. Solution? "Make the cockpit cover of one large and one small piece hinged with a stainless-steel piano hinge. The small one can be folded back to get to the engine controls." I then thought to prevent it from shifting, I could install wooden stops on the inside of the cockpit so the cover would fit tightly against the cockpit sides, flush with the deck.

"We could use the cover as a table," Cindy suggested. To support the table I bought aluminum table fittings, the kind used in camper vans, and had them hard anodized. I installed them with one recessed end in the bottom of the cockpit, and the other recessed end on the underside of the small hinged piece of the cover. To use the table, we would simply lift the small hinged piece up and over so it lay down-side-up atop the larger piece.

The table could be set aside while the raft was removed. I placed a three-inch aluminum tube into the recessed fitting at the bottom of the cockpit and inverted the cover over the top end of this tube, so the table could be swiveled around to suit our needs.

With only two weeks before departure, we went bananas. There wasn't time to run in the evenings because we had to practice navigation, splice anchor line, or do some odd job that had been neglected.

One evening, while discussing coral reefs and landing on coral shores, I said, "To inflate our raft at each island is going to be time-consuming and we might ram it on sharp coral. Inflatable's fine for diving or when we need to haul groceries or fuel, but I might as well face it, we need a hard dinghy as a general, all-purpose, ship-to-shore tender for the tropics."

"We better go measure," We drove to *Xiphias*. The dinghy couldn't go atop the cabin because it would provide too much surface to the wind and seas and would obstruct our view from the cockpit. But the distance from mast to bowsprit bits measured seven feet. Bingo!

We went below and, suddenly, the realization that we'd soon be living our dream intoxicated us. As we stood in the aisle, Cindy clasped my hand. "We're going to have a wonderful passage with light seas and fair winds. I know it."

I pressed her warm body close and kissed her soft, moist lips. "I love you, Cindy. As long as we're together everything life brings will be beautiful."

To the imaginary roll and pitch of *Xiphias* in a seaway, we made love. Finally, the seas quieted, and we held each other, perhaps never closer.

After school the next day, I searched for a hard, fiberglass dinghy and finally found what I liked, a six-foot, eight-inch Montgomery. I delivered a wheeling-dealing speech, telling the clerk that because I'd be taking it out of the country, I shouldn't have to pay sales tax and that I could buy a cheaper one in Long Beach. The clerk seemed convinced, and I carted the dinghy to the marina, where another boat owner helped me carry it. As we neared *Xiphias*, he said that he, too, had a Montgomery, but then I learned he'd paid less than I had, and had bought his right off the showroom floor. So much for my fast-talking, wheeler-dealing!

The dinghy fit and sat no higher than the existing cabin structure. Although it was a bit snug on either side of the Montgomery to work the staysail, I figured that might be an advantage in rough conditions. Then I could wedge myself between the dinghy and a lifeline while changing or dropping sails.

That completed the last major item on the list. Only provisions remained. We'd decided to store 75 pounds of ice and 10 pounds of dry ice in the five-cubic-foot icebox, thinking that should keep food fresh for more than a week. We made a list, adding canned goods of every kind. The list lengthened and by page four, we threw it out.

"Hell, let's just go to the market and buy what we feel like," I said, so daily, after school, we shopped, bringing back boxes of canned and dry foods. Unpacking each box, we stowed items on board, keeping a detailed list of how many of what was stored where (Later this proved to be extremely helpful when we couldn't remember where we'd put the canned curried chicken).

"There's not even space left to fit in a box of matches," Cindy said, "so what about the onions?" Okay, 50 pounds might have been excessive, but we love onions. I rationalized by saying, "Eventually we'll use them and they do keep well." We ended up leaving them in their bag and shoving that into the forepeak.

Now was countdown time. Two days until we depart. Friends at the marina, where we moored *Xiphias*, invited Cindy, the children, and me to dinner, and as we walked down the dock to their yacht, people jumped out yelling, "Surprise." Our friends had organized a "marina" farewell dinner and to top it off everyone had contributed money to buy us a Nicopress tool with assorted sleeves, so we could repair any broken wire rigging. They also handed over the extra money they'd collected. It was overwhelming. We talked of the past, fantasized about the future, and drank. I never emptied my glass of Scotch because while I was busy gabbing, someone always poured in a bit more. When I found I wasn't walking completely straight I blamed it on the tears in my eyes, tears of happiness and sadness as I hugged and kissed everybody. In the early morning, Cindy said, "It's time to take you home."

I didn't argue. I should have left hours ago, and when I woke, I knew I should have left much earlier. My head felt nailed to the pillow and I couldn't move it without suffering excruciating pain. My mouth tasted like the dredging from the bay, unsuccessfully wiped away with cotton balls.

"Ooooooooh," but I received no sympathy, for the other side of the bed was empty. I struggled into my pants and shuffled into the kitchen where Cindy perked coffee. At the table, Ashley and Chris ate cereal. They said nothing, just watched me with condemning eyes as I lurched towards them. In a voice, louder than necessary, Ashley said, "Boy, Roger, you sure got drunk last night. You ran around kissing all the girls and the boys too."

"Boat, sick?" Chris asked through a mouthful of some kind of crunchy something.

I made the chair and through blurred eyes, I squinted at Ashley. "I wasn't kissing everyone," I whispered, "just giving them a loving good-bye hug."

Cindy, still in her robe with her hair slightly mussed, looked gorgeous. She banged a cup of coffee in front of me and said curtly, "Some of those 'hugs' and 'kisses' sure lasted a long time on the pretty ladies." I inhaled Cindy's ever-present scent of soap and started to reach for her.

"What do you want for your last breakfast in this house? Pancakes, waffles, bacon, and eggs?"

Whether she intended or not, the mention of food was punishment enough to make my stomach churn. Mugs padded over to put her head on my lap and then I realized that this might be the final time I'd pet her, that I might never be in this house again, and that months would pass before I saw the children. What about friends, parents? Depressed, I left the table and in the shower, I cried.

But depression was short-lived for on this last day there was too much to do. We stocked the icebox and just after lunch, Mom, Dad, my brother Ron and his wife drove in. We got them settled into a hotel just as my closest friend Jerry and his wife Brenda arrived from San Francisco.

That night we held a grand party with friends, my relatives, and Cindy's relatives. We ate lots, drank little, and shared old stories. After everyone left, Cindy and I went to my parents' room, for I felt compelled to spend a little more time with family.

We reviewed our plans and emphasized how safe the cruise would be.

Ron and Jerry, both sailors, understood the principles of sailing and the safety of a well-founded boat, regardless of its size. Although they added their comments, I felt Mom and Dad's anxiety, their belief that I was on a suicidal voyage. While they said they trusted my decision to sail around the world, I sensed their hope that this was just another new thrill that would quickly end.

For hours we laughed and talked as I tried to allay their fears, instill confidence, and express my love. I told my parents that I loved them deeply and that they were flawless. In this night alive with emotion none of us doubted the others' love. I felt cleansed, glad those I cared for so completely, knew how I felt.

It was late when we got to Cindy's house, but we were hyped and couldn't sleep. So, we discussed my parents and brother. "I've never seen a family as close as yours," she said. "I'll confess that I'm envious."

I held her and changed the subject to our future. While I spun dreams of what we'd see and do, she fell asleep, so she didn't hear me whisper, "I love you, darling," nor did she see me stare toward the window where I waited for the dawn.

Chapter 5
Crossing the Pacific, & the Marquesas Islands in French Polynesia

Cindy sails with me across the Pacific to the Marquesas, French Polynesia, 3,200 nautical miles in 22 days.

We left late in the afternoon and sailed directly to the Marquesas in French Polynesia. However, we had drank a bit too much champagne at our send-off party, so we decided to heave-to or just stop sailing for the night and get some sleep. Early the next morning I thought we were against a cliff because there was just a huge gray wall on our port side. It took some time to realize it was a Navy aircraft carrier. I hailed them on channel 16 to tell them that I had turned off the radio when we went to sleep. They were just concerned about us because we did not respond to their call. I felt embarrassed for turning off channel 16 as it should always be left on, at least in the shipping lanes.

It took us 22 days and we averaged about 6 knots for the entire trip. This is a remarkable average speed for a 28-foot sailboat. However, the reason was, our speed knot log was only reading about half our actual speed, but my navigation said differently.

Something I learned early on during a long passage is that a man should sit to pee or it will end up all over the cabin sole (floor).

I had my ham radio license and Cindy had a friend named Jim who could keep us informed of the weather and connect us by phone to Cindy's mother and her kids. This proved to be a great benefit for years to come.

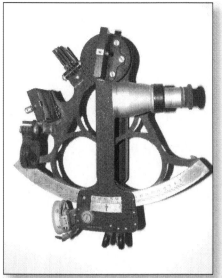

In those days there was no GPS, so I had to navigate by celestial navigation, using a sextant to measure the angle from the horizon to a star, the sun, or a planet. Then I would look up this information in an annual almanac and tables of the celestial body I used to take the sight. This would give me an idea of where we "should" be, but there was no way to be sure when you are in the middle of the ocean with nothing in sight for 22 days.

The horizon had to be visible, so I could not shoot a celestial body at night, but I could do it very early in the morning or just after sunset Then I would shoot the sun mid-day and in the afternoon. Sometimes, I could get a planet just after sunset. The problem was if there were too many clouds or a rainy day, I could not see any celestial bodies or the horizon. We had to keep a close track of our compass course and speed to guess where we were until I could get another sight. So for the entire crossing of the Pacific, we did not know for sure, where we were but we kept track of where we "thought" we were on our chart.

One night I was sure I saw a brightly lit cruise ship. I tried to radio it on channel 16 just to let them know I was there. However, I soon discovered it was a bright half-moon rising over the horizon. It was common to see ships that were not there or even islands that were clouds.

There is one thing about being in the middle of the ocean; if the night sky is clear, there is nothing so beautiful as looking at the millions of stars that could not be seen if anywhere near land. I studied many constellations so I knew which of the stars I could shoot for my navigation.

When we reached, what we thought, was the equator, we celebrated because now we were considered "Shellbacks." This is

the name given to anyone who crosses the equator at sea for the first time. I put on a tie and suit coat and opened a bottle of champagne. Then I climbed up into the hollow of the mainsail to celebrate and Cindy took a photo.

We took turns standing watch in 2-hour shifts each night. There were too many dangers that could happen or that we could hit if we both went to sleep. We were tired all the time and took turns sleeping during the day. We learned after the first two weeks that we could get more sleep by standing 3-hour watches.

Up to that time, we had only taken saltwater baths, which left our skin and hair sticky or feeling even worse than no bath. We did not have a bath as such, we used buckets full of saltwater. I did have a shower, but we only carried 55 gallons of fresh water and we had no idea how long it would take us to reach the Marquesas.

One day, Cindy said to celebrate she would be taking a saltwater bath, but she would rinse in freshwater. I explained that I was not sure where we were, and we need fresh water to drink. It made no difference; she took her bath and freshwater rinse. I decided to do the same, but I was going to use the water from our melted ice in the icebox. We normally threw it overboard or down the sink. When I finished, Cindy crawled up into the mainsail pocket and said she was not coming down until I rinsed that horrible smell of carrots or something off me. Reluctantly, I did a freshwater rinse and cannot remember ever feeling so good. My hair was soft, my skin was smooth, and we had no odors at all.

We continued to sail for another week or so. Not sure where we were or if my celestial navigation was right. After 21 days at sea, I told Cindy, "If I am right, we should see land tomorrow in that direction." I pointed slightly to the right of our present course.

Before dark, we saw a coconut floating by our boat. Then we saw birds that were another sign we were close to land. We were anxious for the sun to rise the next morning, but when it did we saw nothing but open ocean, just like we had seen for the last three weeks.

It was about noon when we saw the very tip of our first sight of an island. As we got closer, we saw other islands, but we were still not sure which island we were approaching. At least I knew my celestial navigation was right and we were heading directly into the Marquesas....or some other islands.

We continued following our course and it looked like we would be approaching the island at night. So, we decided to drop all sails and wait until sunrise before attempting to enter. There was no sleeping that night.

At first light, we approached the island and began to follow the coastline looking for an anchorage or town. I looked at our charts closely to try to determine which island we were at. As we continued, we realized we had reached our expected destination of Nuku Hiva. Somehow, we had missed Hatutu, Motu One, and Motu Iti islands but we arrived safely.

We found the town and spent at least two weeks exploring this beautiful island. There were five other cruising boats anchored in the bay. We met them all and they were all friendly and welcoming. One was from France with two children. We seemed to hit it off with them and kept in touch for a few years as we cruised.

This bay was beautiful with calm water and a sandy bottom for anchoring. We made it a point to walk around as much as we could. The locals were very friendly. We had to officially check into French Polynesia at this point.

We discovered many other beautiful bays on the island. Some were too rough to anchor so we would find another more protected one, and walk over to take photos.

Almost daily, we would see someone banging an octopus against the rocks to soften the muscle, so it was not so tough.

It was here that I attempted to open my first coconut. I broke my heavy dive knife trying to pry through the thick tough husk to reach the nut with coconut and coconut water inside.

We were soon approached by some locals who laughed at me and offered to show me the easy way to shell the husk of coconuts using just a sharp stick, they called an "Oh." They stuck one end in the ground. Then they thrust the coconut husk down hard onto the sharp end of the stick, rolling the coconut to one side so it would pry off the husk at that spot. Then they continued this procedure to remove the rest of the husk. They could get to the nut within a minute. Then, to crack open the nut, they would take the back, dull end of a machete, and bang it in the center of the coconut, rotating as they hit it. The coconut would crack in the center and break into two halves.

Even though they spoke French, not English, they explained that every coconut, papaya, fruit, etc. belonged to someone. The people were extremely courteous as they attempted to explain this to us. We were supposed to get permission to take anything off the trees or even off the ground.

From Nuku Hiva, we continued to Ua Huka, Ua Pou, Fatu Huku, Hiva Oa, Tahuata, Molopu (Mohotani), and Motu Nao spending our last anchorage in the Marquesas at Fatu Hiva.

Before leaving on our cruise, I was advised to read a book by Thor Heyerdahl that was about the Marquesas. He was a famous Norwegian who was most famous for his book and the story of sailing the *"Kon Tiki"* across oceans. I had brought the book with me and read it during our passage. It was entitled *"Fatu Hiva"* after the island where we were to anchor for the night.

The book was about him and his wife wanting to leave Norway in 1936 to escape Norwegian civilization and go in search of a place where they could live as the natives did hundreds of years ago. He was a biologist and anthropologist. He fell in love with the Marquesas, especially Fatu Hiva where they built a bamboo house and he began to learn as much as he could about the primitive people who lived there. His book ended with them hiding in a cave on the side of a mountain looking for a ship that he and his wife could board to leave the islands. It was apparent he was afraid of the locals. It was a bit mysterious because there was no real reason given as to why he was so frightened.

While anchored in the deep bay of Fatu Hiva, we were approached by a man in a canoe. He said he had a telegram for Cindy. Both our legs went weak; something must have happened to the children. Cindy refused to open it, so I did. The message was from the local airline. We had tried to book Cindy on a flight to Papeete, Tahiti from Nuka Hiva but the small plane was mostly full of French officials. Nevertheless, we put her name on the waiting list. So now if we motored for two days upwind, she could catch that flight. She decided to continue with me to Tahiti. We radioed back to Jim who connected us to her mother and children.

She explained everything and that she might be one or two weeks late getting back home.

The man who delivered the telegram was from the next town, about three miles away. He was the local policeman for the entire island. He had paddled his dugout canoe over to this bay to deliver the message. We invited him aboard and gave him a cup of coffee and some sweets. I asked him how he knew where we were, that we were anchored in this bay of Fatu Hiva. He explained that in the Marquesas, each island has a short-wave radio and they keep track of where each cruising yacht is anchored and report it to the authorities in Papeete.

I asked him about the mysterious underground lake and sacred burial grounds I had read about in the book, *Fatu Hiva*. He said we could visit the underground lake, but we could not enter the underwater cave to the sacred area. He was adamant about this. He explained that Thor Heyerdahl had entered this sacred area and had removed some of the remains of their ancient ancestors. The people were really upset with him because he knew it was not permitted for ANYONE to enter this sacred cave. Ah, now I knew why his book ended as it did.

The next morning, we raised the anchor and moved closer to the location where the underground lake was located. It took some time to set the anchor because the bottom was solid coral. I finally got the anchor set but knew I would have to dive down to get it out of the coral when we left.

We went ashore on the rocks and the cliff and began searching for the entrance into this mysterious underground lake. For hours we searched but could not find it. We were about to give up when a small hole in the side of the cliff was revealed. We entered it slowly because it was so dark inside.

It took some time for our eyes to adjust to the light. This was not a lake but a small pond. The water was fresh and warm, so we took off our clothes and went for a dip. I thought I knew where the underwater entrance was to the sacred area, but I had no intention of trying to find it. It would only cause me more temptation to go get my fins, mask, and an underwater flashlight.

After several hours of enjoying the warm freshwater, we returned to *Xiphias*. When we got there, the bow was tilted down and the stern high. I realized my chain had wrapped around other coral heads and was being pulled under the coral. When the tide rose, the chain was taught, thus pulling it down. We went aboard. I started the engine, let out some chain to take the tension off, grabbed my face mask, and dove in. It was shallow, and no wind was blowing so it was not difficult to free the chain and anchor. We motored back to where we had originally anchored and decided to stay for a few more days before leaving for the Tuamotus, and then on to Papeete where my Cindy would have to leave.

Chapter 6
The Tuamotus to American Samoa

Ahe in the Tuamotus and Tahiti in French Polynesia. Suwarrow in the Cook Islands then on to Pago Pago, and American Samoa: *Learning to catch fish and octopus by hand then cooking them in coconut milk. We witness a plane destroy a hotel in Pago Pago, American Samoa. However, it never touched the hotel. We leave Pago Pago in fear for our lives*

It took us just over one week to sail to the Tuamotus from the Marquesas. The day we left, the wind was light and behind us and the seas were calm. We had high hopes for a pleasant sail to these coral atolls. Unfortunately, the weather was not cooperative after the first day.

The sky was full of clouds with rain and squalls. I couldn't get a good navigational site for the entire trip. We knew by our speed and course we should be close. The Tuamotus are just a lot of low coral atolls only as high as the tallest tree so we had to be close before we could see one of the atolls.

After the first five days, we stayed up all night sailing as slowly as we could hoping we would see or hear something in the dark before we ran into a coral reef.

It was in the middle of the night when we heard the breakers before we saw the shadow of what looked like an atoll. We started the motor and motored back the way we came slowly and waited until daylight.

At daylight, we saw the coral atoll we had heard during the night. It did not take us long to find the passage into the lagoon. This matched our chart and showed that the atoll was Ahe.

The channel was narrow, and the tide was ebbing or coming out of the pass. I climbed the mast so I could see where we were going and look for any dangers. Cindy motored *Xiphias* at nearly full throttle to make forward progress. I had set the depth alarm for 10 feet. The engine began to overheat, and the alarm sounded but we could not turn around in the narrow passage. Then the depth alarm went off and I was sure we were in for a major disaster or damage. I studied the water looking for deeper water, but it all looked the same. Finally, near the end of the pass, the water turned to a darker blue, the depth alarm stopped, and Cindy could cut back on the throttle. Now both alarms were off. The first thing I saw was a bunch of coral heads just reaching the surface. We could see a beach with trees and a small village on the other side of the lagoon.

I stayed up the mast to keep a close watch for the coral heads as we motored toward the village. I would yell down to Cindy which direction to steer in order to miss these dangers. We learned that the sun should be high and slightly behind us to see clearly. When we got there, the village was surrounded by a reef. I climbed down the mast and took over the helm. By slowly motoring parallel to the lagoon we found a shallow entrance. There was a bamboo pole stuck in the sand on either side. We only had about two feet under our keel. Inside, the anchorage was well-protected with a sand bottom that would make for good anchor holding. Now we were positive we had arrived at Ahe atoll. We saw another, much larger boat also anchored in the same area.

The boat was from Lichtenstein, the smallest country in Europe. As soon as we set the anchor the couple rowed over to introduce themselves. They were very friendly and offered to show us some of the reefs, and how to dive when there are sharks in the water. I learned quickly and saw many sharks but decided I did not have the courage my European friend did. After a few days they left but I knew we would see them again because they were headed to Australia as was I.

We met a Frenchman and his girlfriend who were living in the little village. They both spoke great English. He was staying in a small grass house that was right next to the small house that belonged to Bernard Moitessier, a famous French sailor and writer.

He offered to make us a dinner of octopus cooked in fresh coconut milk. He explained that after killing the octopus by turning its head inside out, he would drag it across the coral and rocks to get rid of the slimy membrane that gave the octopus its strong taste. Then he beat it with a stick to make the meat more tender. He showed us how easy it was to make coconut milk. As in the Marquesas, he shed the thick husk by thrusting the coconut onto the sharp end of a stick in the ground, then cracking the nut with a machete. He had a grater to remove the coconut inside each half. This grater was no more than about ¾ of a 2-inch circle of flat steel with a bunch of teeth cut or ground around the outside. The grater was attached to a board he would sit on and then pass the inside of the coconut over the grater to make coconut the size of sand. Then he put this grated coconut into a fine cloth and twisted it and squeezed until white, sweet milk dripped out into a bowl.

First, he boiled the octopus and cut it into fine pieces. On an open fire, he fried sliced potatoes and onions. When they were nearly done, he added the octopus pieces and the coconut milk. This he simmered for a few minutes then served it. It was wonderful. I have used this recipe many times throughout my life.

We learned a lot from this young Frenchman. He taught us how to catch fish by hand. He would wait until the tide was low then go to a special place on the reef where there were many fish swimming in the small puddles left on top of the reef. He showed us how to catch and kill the octopus and much more.

Our time was running short for Cindy to get home so after a week we reluctantly left for Papeete, Tahiti. After we said our goodbyes, we motored across the lagoon to the pass, but we found the tide coming in, and along with it was a strong incoming current. We decided to anchor next to the pass for the night and leave the next morning when the tide should be slack. This worked perfectly and we had a comfortable sail to Tahiti.

When we arrived, we anchored *Xiphias* between two boats near the shore. Since there was little room, I had to set two anchors off the bow, one to port and one to starboard so it would prevent the bow from moving left or right. The stern had to be tied to two separate bollards or posts to keep the stern from moving side to side. After we were securely anchored, we relaxed and had a good night's sleep.

Early the next morning we went to the airport and booked Cindy's flight home to California. Unfortunately, the next day she left and I was alone. She planned on returning to see me, without the children, in Pago Pago, American Samoa. I had to plan carefully to make sure I had enough time to get there before she arrived.

My time in Papeete, Tahiti was both good and bad. I loved the people and the local natives. But there were strong squalls that frequently caused boats to drag their anchors.

One night there was a bad storm outside the breakwater. My neighbor to the left, in a boat name *Mintaka*, sat out on deck watching the huge waves come through the pass. I made myself a drink and went out on my bow to watch as well. I introduced myself, his name was Charles, and his wife was Nita. We talked about how high the waves were breaking across the pass. They must have been near or more than 50-feet high. Fortunately, further down the breakwater, other passes did not have breaking water. This is where all the local fishing boats returned to safety inside the harbor.

Suddenly, the big boat that took tourists and supplies to the nearby island of Moorea, was attempting to enter the main pass. I thought to myself, "this is suicidal, or the skipper knows what he is doing." I watched and lost sight of it in the trough of a wave then it came straight up on the crest of the next wave and buried its bow into the water. Then it pitch-poled or turned over with the stern going over its bow. Within moments, it was upside-down banging against the breakwater. Instantly, there were harbor boats and fishing boats there to rescue as many as they could. As I watched this happen, I began to worry, if the wind shifted a little, those big waves would be coming right at us.

Just after dark, the wind shifted, and we had the wind coming from our starboard and waves coming straight at us through the pass. I felt safe because I had set two anchors off the bow. It would take a lot to make them drag.

I heard a scream from my right and went on deck to see what had happened. I saw the boat that was anchored several boats upwind, to my right had hit the rocks and the woman was screaming for help. Before we could do anything, the harbor boat tossed them a heavy line and quickly towed it off the rocks out into the middle of the bay. When he did this, somehow the anchor that was being towed behind him tripped my starboard bow anchor. Immediately, I began to bang into *Mintaka* to my left. As I tried to pull in my anchor to reset it, my anchor windlass broke from too much strain. Now I was in trouble. Charles kept hanging fenders or inflatable rubber balls between us to reduce the damage.

Out of nowhere, a small rowboat approached my side and offered to help. No words were exchanged, a man and a woman boarded my boat. I asked them to cast off the stern lines and I attempted to motor forward. As soon as I was past *Mintaka*, to my left, the wind shoved me over his anchor line and my prop wrapped around it and the motor died. I immediately grabbed my face mask and underwater flashlight and dove into the water. My prop had about three wraps of *Mintaka's* anchor line around it. I tried my best to unwrap it, but it was so taught, there was no way. My boat was going up and down about 5 to 6 feet with each wave. When I surfaced, I yelled at Charles that I had wrapped his anchor line around my prop. I asked him if he could let out only a few feet then pull in the slack as soon as I had released it from my prop. He was reluctant because he was too close to the rocks behind him. I explained that his boat and mine would both be on the rocks if he did not give me some slack.

I told him to count to five after I went underwater, let out about 3 to 4 feet then pull it back in. As I dove down, I felt the slack and quickly unwrapped his anchor line from my prop. Just then, my stern raised high and fast and then came down on my head and right shoulder. I blacked out. The next thing I knew someone had a hold of my hand asking me if I was alright. With his help, I managed to get back aboard and realize what had happened. The guy and his wife, who had come to help me had grabbed my hand when it broke the surface. He had grabbed it and held on. They helped me re-anchor my boat and then left to look after their boat. They told me their boat name was *Vela*. I promised I would come by and thank them when this was all over. I was now anchored in the middle of the bay, which was illegal, and *Mintaka* looked like it was anchored firmly. I looked at my boat and there was some damage, but it was mostly woodwork that I could repair. Tomorrow I would check out *Mintaka* to see how badly she was damaged.

The next morning, in the calm, I surveyed the damage done to both boats. Fortunately, he had a big, thick wooden rub rail running the length of his boat that took most of the damage. It took me about a week to repair their boat and bring her back to where it was before the damage. They were happy with the results and even said the repairs were better than it was originally. We became good friends and planned to meet in New Zealand. I had all the time in the world to repair *Xiphias* which was not too severely damaged.

As soon as I could, I searched out the people on *Vela* that had helped me. Without their help, I would probably not be here. I found *Vela* about five to six boats to my right. The boat flew a flag from Denmark. When I met them, it was apparent they were Danish but spoke nearly perfect English. They were a young handsome pair and we became instant friends.

I visited them regularly over the next few weeks. They had a cat that they enjoyed because it was smart and kept them company. I commented that maybe that is what I needed, a cat. The next day they brought me a kitten and a litter box.

Now I had a companion so I would not be so lonely. I called Cindy and told her about our new crew member. She said the kids would love it. I also mentioned that I needed a name for him, and I wanted her and the children to give it a name. Cindy said that it was a male kitten. Perhaps I should name it "Pintle," after the male part that holds the outboard rudder to the boat. If it had been a female kitten she would have been named "Gudgeon," the female part that holds the male piece.

One morning I was approached by a local Polynesian who introduced himself as Joe. He spoke four languages. He wanted to learn as much as he could about my language and the United States. He invited me to his house that was built out of local trees and a type of grass roof. He and his wife were as kind as anyone could be. They wanted nothing from me but to learn. I spent most of my time with this friendly couple learning as much about their culture as they learned about mine.

One thing I learned was that some of the men do not get circumcised, but instead get what he called a sub-circumcision. This is where they cut the top of the foreskin, so it folds back but is not removed. Some other customs were not so unique, and many are changing.

I met a great guy named Jim, who wanted to sail with me to American Samoa. I had to be sure I got there before Cindy arrived, but we had plenty of time. So, we sailed through all the islands of French Polynesia, then on to the Cook Islands where we anchored at Suwarrow Island for a week.

No one lived there but there was an old shack where an airplane spotter was stationed during the war. He had stayed there after the war and recently got ill and had to leave, never to return. He must have been an old man by that time.

He left a message for anyone who visited, to feed his chickens and look after his place until he returned. There were still a few chickens left. I presumed other boats had been there and eaten the chickens. He even wrote a recipe on how to smoke fish using his smoker that he made from an old 44-gallon drum using the local wood for the smoke. His message also mentioned to please leave something that he or others who visited his place could use. Jim and I decided we would leave something but were not sure just what it would be yet.

We found the fishing excellent right off the back of the boat. A short distance across the lagoon we found many oysters and giant coconut crabs. The body of these crabs must have been 8 inches across, and their pinchers were as large as my fist. Since these coconut crabs eat mostly coconuts, their meat tastes of coconut so we grabbed one with a small hand net and collected a bunch of oysters, and took them back to the anchorage.

Jim and I collected a lot of the local wood and put it in the smoker and followed the directions. Jim smoked the oysters and fish while I cooked the crabs and made some coconut milk. I fried some onions and potatoes to go with all of it. I think Pintle enjoyed the whole event as much as we did because he would not stay off our backs the entire time, we prepared the oysters and fish. He got more than his share.

We knew we had to get underway soon. Jim and I wanted to leave something as requested in the note. We found a huge, old anchor wedged under the rocks where we were anchored. This would make a perfect mooring. We attached a bit of chain with a shackle and let some rope to the surface. I used a bunch of empty coconut shells, tied together as a float. I would use it if I just arrived, but I would dive on it first to make sure it was secure.

While anchored at Suwarrow Island, we heard on the single-sideband radio, a warning about typhoon (hurricane) *Claudia*, heading our way. It was not clear exactly where it was right now because there was a Japanese station that interrupted the exact latitude and longitude, but from what we could make out, it was headed our way.

Pago Pago, American Samoa has a far safer, better protected, anchorage than Suwarrow when or if the typhoon hit. We did not have the time to wait to find out for sure, but it sounded like it was close to our location. I had to get to American Samoa to meet my Cindy so we left, hoping we could beat the typhoon.

On our second night out, we got caught in what we thought was the typhoon because the winds were blowing about 50 knots and the waves were high. We "hove-to" (reduce sail area and backwind the jib, then move the tiller in the opposite direction) so the boat would remain in one place pointing about 60 to 70 degrees to the wind. It was a rough, frightening night. We thought we were at the beginning of the cyclone and the worst was yet to come.

That night, I regretted not setting my parachute anchor instead because it would be impossible to go forward if the conditions got worse.

The next morning things were better, so we took off again for Samoa. The wind and seas continued to lessen, and we eventually made it to Pago Pago just one day before Cindy's arrival. As we entered the long, deep, narrow channel, we passed under a gondola that must take people across the channel to the other side that was mountainous. This gondola had to go from ground level or ocean level up high to the other side. We continued up the channel and passed a smelly fish factory that must have thrown all their rubbish into the channel for it was filthy.

Finally, we saw other boats anchored and some on moorings. We anchored close to shore so we would not have to row far. Then we caught some needed sleep.

The next morning, we went ashore and met some of the other cruisers in a local café. They informed us that we were lucky because we had only caught the edge of the typhoon. It had rapidly dropped from a full typhoon to a tropical storm.

After we left the café, I went directly to the Rainmaker Hotel to book a room for Cindy and me for five nights. Jim could stay on the boat. Cindy was to arrive tomorrow so Jim and I made it a point to take hot showers before he returned to the boat. I spent the first night in the hotel and found it a real treat to have a soft bed and a nice restaurant for meals.

The next afternoon, I went to the airport and met Cindy. She looked gorgeous but she was exhausted from the long flight and had jet lag. We both took showers, had dinner in the hotel restaurant, and went to bed. The next day we began our tour to see as much of Pago Pago as we could in the few days she had left. We enjoyed every hour of the rest of our time together. We even took the gondola to the top of the other side of the channel. We rented a taxi to show us the rest of the small island. The days passed too quickly until it was time for her to return home. We went to the airport and waited for her plane. Just before it arrived, Cindy promised she would return with the children in Fiji and try to live my dream with me, but she still was not sure. She had two children to consider.

Shortly after Cindy left, there was going to be a big celebration. The night before it was to begin, Jim and I were having a drink in the bar at the only local hotel. There was a group of Americans who were half-drunk talking about what they were going to do for the big celebration.

As we spoke with them, they explained that they had flown a special plane over from Hawaii to drop skydivers over the crowd of people. There were four skydivers, two pilots, and a navigator. The skydivers would set off smoke flares as they free-fell from a considerable altitude. They commented on how difficult this might be because there were mountains all around and the deep entrance channel into the harbor. They were experienced and exuded confidence it would all go as planned.

One of the pilots proudly said that after the skydivers jumped out of the plane, he would do a U-turn and fly out of the channel by going under the gondola cables.

The next day Jim and I went ashore to watch the event. The problem was that the day was overcast so the skydivers could not jump from the planned altitude but below clouds which left little, if any, time to deploy their flares.

As the plane passed overhead, two of the four skydivers jumped out and only had time to open their parachutes and land exactly where they were supposed to. Then the plane made a second pass but this time they seemed too close to the top of the mountain. The other two jumped but only had time to open their chutes before they landed in the trees. Immediately we heard sirens as the ambulance and firetruck headed up to where they had fallen.

The pilot's plan to fly under the gondola went horribly wrong. The tail section caught the cable and the plane crashed into the center compound of the "U" shaped hotel, missing the hotel entirely.

Jim and I ran there to see if we could help but it was apparent the only ones who were killed were those in the airplane and one man standing where it crashed. The hotel was undamaged. However, there was burning debris on top of the roof of each wing of the hotel.

We watched as the local firemen arrived and ran their hoses to put out the fire. Unfortunately, they did not seem to have the right ends to connect one hose to another so there was a lot of reversing ends. Then when the water was finally turned on, there were knots in the hose. None of them worked. Some of the hoses burst. There was still time because there were only a few small pieces of burning debris on the hotel roofs.

There was a lot of confusion. The hotel was still open, so Jim and I thought about going inside and having a drink while we watched the chaos going on outside. I told Jim to go on in, I would join him later. I wanted to watch the "keystone" firemen in action.

Then about six men carried a big pump to the swimming pool to use it to shoot water on the roof to put out the burning debris. No one knew how to start the pump. The hotel slowly burnt to the ground, but the office and bar remained open during this whole event. I went in and had a drink with Jim. Those of us that were there all talked about how fortunate it was that there were no guests in the rooms or the ones that were there, had plenty of time to get out.

Later that same day, we heard the skydivers were alright, but bruised and cut from falling into the trees; nothing serious. Their main problem was how to explain what happened to the plane when they got back to Hawaii.

We met a local Samoan who was really from Western Samoa, not American Samoa. He was a security guard at a small local mall just outside of town. He told us he could get me a bag of marijuana for $25 but he needed the money upfront. So, I gave him the money and we scheduled a time we would meet him ashore to pick up my ounce of weed.

When we went in to meet him on the scheduled day and time, he was not there so we waited an hour and returned to the boat. A few more days passed and nothing. Then one evening, he waved at me from shore. I went in to pick up what I had paid for, but he said he wanted to come to my boat. There we smoked one joint or marijuana cigarette together with Jim. He handed me three more rolled joints. I asked him for the ounce I had paid for. He said he would give me even more for another $10. He explained that it had been a bad season and there was not much available. I gave him another $10 and he promised me he would be back the next evening. We waited and waited, still nothing. We waited three more days, still nothing.

I do not like to get ripped off by anyone for any amount of money, so I decided to get even; I knew where he worked. We went to the mall and he was not working that day. I asked to speak to the mall manager. I told him we were from National Geographic and I was doing a story on an American Samoan family. I had loaned him $25 and another $10, then I found out he was from Western Samoa so all my time had been wasted and I was out the $35. The manager gave me the money and told me he would take it out of his paycheck and have a long talk about it and see if he should even work there.

As we were heading back to my boat some friends on another boat called me over and introduced me to a huge American Samoan who was willing to sell me a bag of marijuana for $10. I told him my story about the other guy and he got really mad. He told me that he was the only grower on the island and if this guy was going to sell me any marijuana, he was stealing it off his land.

He told me he knew the guy and would take care of him. I was not sure what he meant by "take care of him" but in Pago Pago, nothing is out of the realm of possibilities. This is not what I wanted but realized it was too late. I imagined this guy with broken legs or something similar. No matter what happened, he would want to get even with us. Hell, he could shoot at us from the land.

The next morning it was still blowing hard, but we figured we were safer at sea than we were waiting for this guy to get even, so we checked out of American Samoa and headed for Western Samoa.

Chapter 7
Western Samoa to Fiji

Western Samoa, friendly people, and very modern for a small pacific island with beautiful beaches and waterfalls that one can slide down to the bottom far below. The Tonga Islands have special customs and we participated in a few.

Jim and I went ashore and checked into Western Samoa. The capital was Apia and it looked modern but small. We walked around town talking to the locals who told us about the "Sliding Rock Falls." We took a taxi to a river that was famous for its slippery rocks where one could slide down the

long stretch of river on the steep, smooth rocks and not get hurt. Well, almost not get hurt. It was difficult to maintain any kind of control on the way down and impossible to stop or slow down. Jim hit his head badly but not bad enough to need medical care. We spent the day sliding down the rocks and climbing back up to do it again and again.

After a week in Western Samoa, we headed to the Tonga Islands. This was a safe anchorage and there were lots of islands to visit. The people were

friendly. The men wore lap-laps which are a woven material around their waste. This lap-lap custom was passed down from generation to generation.

We spent several nights eating on land with the locals. We watched the women catch octopus and turn its head inside out to kill it. This was going to be part of our dinner.

They made a fire out of wood in a large hole in the ground. While the fire was burning, they wrapped the fish, octopus, and other seafood they wanted to eat, in banana leaves with coconut milk. Then, when the fire burnt down to coals, they would put the wrapped food on top of the hot coals and cover the hole with dirt. After about two hours they dug away the dirt and removed the food in the banana leaves and served it to us. The taste of everything was fantastic.

After visiting many of the Tonga islands and diving in underwater caves, we left for Fiji where Cindy and her two children were to meet me. We had a great sail with plenty of wind and moderate seas.

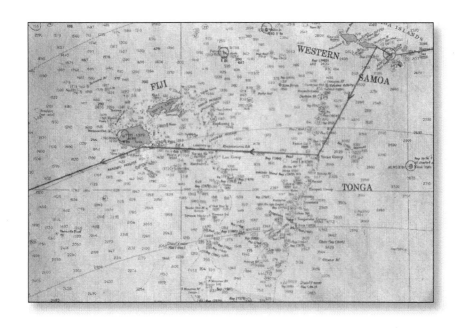

Chapter 8
New Caledonia to New Zealand

Cindy and her two children join me in Fiji. We visit the outer islands and meet awesome locals then we leave for New Caledonia on our way to New Zealand.

The morning we were to arrive in Fiji, I had the early morning watch and as the sun came up, I saw a reef directly in front of us and the water was only 20 feet deep. I made a quick turn back the way we had come and sailed away from the reef for about an hour.

Now, I was not sure where we were. I checked the chart and it showed the reef was long but there was a passage through it. But I did not know for sure if it was to the left or right of our current position.

I took a chance and we sailed to our left or port for about two or three hours and saw the passage into Suva, Fiji. It was getting late, so we decided to anchor off a small island for the night then continued to Suva the next morning.

I still had a lot of time before Cindy and her children arrived, so Jim and I toured around Suva and ate some great Indian food. Fiji is full of people from India so most of the stores and restaurants are run by Indians.

After a week, we sailed around to the other end of the island to Nandi where the airport was located. While anchored there, Jim found another boat he could crew on with a nice couple. Much later I learned the guy's wife liked Jim a little too much which ended up causing a great problem during their cruise to Australia.

Thanks to the ham radio I had aboard and my ham license, I kept in touch with a close friend of Cindy's and he would connect us by phone. I was always aware of what was happening with her and the time of their arrival.

When they arrived, I was surprised because along with Cindy and her two children, was a close friend of mine accompanied by his far too young girlfriend.

He wanted to surprise me and had asked Cindy not to say anything. So, on my little 28-foot sailboat there were six of us. This was OK for a few days, but we wanted to sail more of the Fijian waters. I know they enjoyed themselves and fortunately, they were there for just over a week, then we said our goodbyes. So now it was just the four of us and that worked out simply fine.

We sailed out to the Yasawa Islands which is a long chain of islands that are close together and all still part of Fiji. We heard there was an island that had a natural cave full of freshwater with underwater passages to other caverns and tunnels.

As soon as we anchored off the village, we had to get permission to enter this cave from the village chief. We had to give him a token of money.

I took my face mask and an underwater flashlight in case the water was clear, and I could explore the underwater caves. We climbed up to the entrance and entered the cavern. We were amazed at what we saw. It was beautiful inside. It was full of water, but one could still walk around the sides. There was a hole in the top that let in light, so it was easy to see around.

After we explored the sides of the cavern, I put on my face mask and entered the water which was crystal clear and about 50 feet deep. I immediately saw a hole about 10 feet down. I dove down and saw it went through into another cavern that had to be full of water as well. It was a short distance to swim through to the other cavern. This one was mostly closed at the top, so it was darker than the other. I felt more comfortable with my underwater flashlight to see more clearly.

I swam around checking it out. Just below the surface, I saw an underwater tunnel that led deep into the mountain. I thought about entering it but realized I was alone, and it could be dangerous. It looked like there were air pockets on the top of the cave so I decided to go in for a short distance and see if I could breathe some of this air. It did not work; the air bubbles were only about ¼ inch from the ceiling so there was no air to breathe. I realized I may have gone in too far, so I immediately turned around and headed back.

I was running out of air, I began to worry that I would not make it. I needed air now. I was at the entrance when I raised my head to grab some air. I did this too soon for I hit it hard on the ceiling right at the entrance. I saw blood in the water but my head was now above water so I could breathe.

I knew it was time to go back to the main cavern where Cindy and the children were waiting. I wished I had brought my SCUBA tank and fins. The return was simple, and my bleeding was not nearly as bad as I thought. Cindy asked me what had happened, so I told her I did something stupid.

We loved Fiji. The locals must have liked our family because we were often invited into their homes to drink kava and have great meals. We learned so much about their culture and their strong belief in magic. One night we were drinking Kava (only men permitted) and slapping our hands, as was the custom, I learned that one of the guys with us was a man of magic. I had to prod him to tell me about his powers.

He waited until he drank more Kava then began to explain to me that there are good and bad magic men and that his and their powers were real. He told me stories of how he had cured people and how he had made others suffer who were bad. Others were sitting with us who told stories of how the magic man had healed their wounds and sicknesses in their families. He was worshiped for his goodness and powers. He was so convincing that I believed him.

After nearly a month, we decided it was time to leave, so we sailed out to the Kadavu islands on our way to New Caledonia. The people of Kadavu were also very friendly and we were invited into their homes. We met one older guy who wanted us to take him back to the main island of Fiji. I tried to explain to him we were not returning to the main island and he got really upset. Another family told us this guy was dangerous because he was their local magic man and they sincerely believed he had strong powers to cause us harm. As we were preparing to leave, he warned us that we had better take him to the main island or we would regret it. We apologized and left for New Caledonia.

Our passage was comfortable, and Ashley and Chris had become used to the boat and its movement. We entered through the back passage into New Caledonia and found some great, protected anchorages with rivers of freshwater cascading down into one of the bays where we were anchored. Cindy took this opportunity and did laundry while I filled our water tanks.

After a few days, we headed into Noumea, the capital and largest town on this, French-owned island. Most of the women wore high heels and dressed like they would in a big city. The place was spotless, and we felt welcomed by anyone we met.

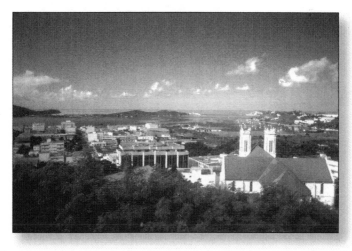

We spent about a week visiting the city then moved to Isle des Pines which was a great anchorage, shallow with a sand bottom. The white sand beaches were gorgeous. There was a town a few miles from the anchorage where we could buy supplies before we left for New Zealand.

While we waited, I taught young Chris how to swim. I showed her how to put on a face mask and use a snorkel. She loved it and would swim alongside me, looking at the fish for hours at a time while Cindy and Ashley would prepare meals or explore the land. We loved Isle des Pines because it was so protected, with clear water and simple beauty.

I listened to the single-sideband radio daily, trying to figure out the best time to leave for New Zealand, an upwind sail. I wanted a weather front to pass between New Zealand and New Caledonia so we would have at least a week of sailing without the wind on our nose. The day came and we had the weather pattern I had been wanting. This gave us about a week with light beam winds.

Chapter 9
New Zealand, a Life Changer

New Zealander's are often known as Kiwis after the Kiwi bird that only exists in New Zealand. They are also famous for their native Mauri people. We love New Zealand and all its people.

*T*he sail was perfect as we sailed into the Bay of Islands on the Northern tip of the North Island of New Zealand. We anchored at *Opua* and immediately made some great friends. One kiwi let us borrow her car so we could see most of the North Island. We bought a couple of tents so we would not have to pay for a hotel.

We visited the 90-mile beach where, at low tide, we found a huge area full of small, live clams. We gathered up a bucket full and took it back to our camp. The campgrounds all had toilets and a group kitchen. We were preparing to cook some clam chowder with all the clams we had gathered. One of the others in the kitchen told us they were called Pippies and most people did not eat them because they were so small and in such abundance. They preferred the larger clams. Mostly the poorer people ate Pippies. However, they watched carefully how we prepared our chowder. They had never heard of clam chowder, so they were curious about what this American family was cooking. When we finished, we passed out samples of our chowder and we were overwhelmed with people asking for our recipe.

We continued our trip around the North Island and fell in love with the country and its people. When we returned to Opua, we moved the boat up a river and put it between two mooring poles that were for all sizes of boats. There was a small town named Keri Keri only a short walk from our mooring spot.

In front of us at our mooring was another American boat, Charles and Nita's *Mintaka*, the boat I had collided with in Papeete, Tahiti We had planned on meeting again in New Zealand, and here we were, moored only boat lengths away from each other.

It was about this time that Cindy began to question my life's objective. Was I going to continue cruising, or would I return home? This discussion went on for weeks. We seemed to be drawing further apart. I wanted to continue living my dream. I wanted Cindy and the kids to continue with me. Cindy wanted to return to the States to educate her children. I fully understood and agreed with the need to educate the children, but we were both teachers and had plenty of time to educate them and they had us full-time to answer questions and help them learn. I was sure they would learn as much if not more with us. I was also sure Cindy and the children would soon be leaving me alone. It was up to me to decide if I wanted to continue living my dream or return home and live like everyone else. Time would tell.

Then one morning while we were moored in the Keri Keri river, Charles came by and asked if I wanted to go to the market with him. Cindy was sewing and did not want to go with us. When we returned, standing on the side of the river with bags full of groceries, Cindy yelled at me. I knew something was wrong by the sound of her voice. Charles took me out to our boat and Cindy was crying saying "She's not here, I looked everywhere." Ashley was standing next to her, so I knew that Chis had fallen into the river. Apparently, she had gone outside to play Captain Hook and tried to climb over the lifelines, down into the small dinghy we used to go ashore. It must have capsized, and she drowned. Cindy was inside sewing and did not hear her fall into the water. She had not been worried about Chris being outside the boat alone because she knew how to swim. She asked Ashley to go out occasionally to check on her. Then Ashley came back inside and said she couldn't find her.

I instantly grabbed my face mask and dove into the water. The current was strong so I knew she could not be here under the boat. I began my search, but I was in a state of panic and could not hold my breath. Shortly, a powerboat came alongside. I could see it was a local named John Woods who was our friend. He was speaking to Cindy. Then he and a few others began looking for Chris. About 15 minutes later they found her floating face down in the middle of the river.

It's difficult to explain the emotions of losing a child. For me, it was like a sense of helplessness, disbelief, and a sensation like a hole in my gut. Cindy had her body cremated and we decided to take her ashes back home to California. Before we left, our New Zealand friend, John Woods organized a memorial service for the little girl and many locals and cruisers attended. It was extremely emotional for all of us, but especially for my Cindy. We were in a living hell. We knew we had to go home as soon as possible because each day we stayed was a reminder.

I had my parents take some money out of my savings and wire it to us so we could buy tickets to get us home. Some other local friends, Keith and Angela made all the arrangements and even drove us to Auckland to catch our flight. We arrived a day early and they insisted we stay with some friends of theirs who would then take us to the airport in the morning.

When we arrived at the airport, the next morning, we heard that the airline had just gone on strike, so our plane was not leaving, but there was another flight about to leave right now. I do not know how, but they knew who we were and our situation. They managed to get us on this last flight out of New Zealand to California. The only problem was that the plane would not be resupplied due to the strike. None of us were very hungry at the moment having just had breakfast, but after the plane was in the air and we were heading home, we wished there had been time to grab even a snack from a machine, as there was no food or drinks for the 18-hour flight.

When we got back to California there was another memorial service for Chris and both our families and friends attended. Friends and family tried to ask what had happened but every time I tried to explain, I broke down and cried. It was too difficult to talk about it because I would relive it in my mind, and as I spoke, I would break down.

After a couple of weeks of this, I told Cindy I had to go back to my boat in New Zealand. Cindy wanted to go back too but I suggested she wait until she was better. Being on the boat would be a constant reminder of the tragedy. She warned me that she may never come back, and I should consider selling *Xiphias* and come home, or else.

I returned to New Zealand alone. As soon as I was aboard, I was constantly reminded of Chris's death. Every time I saw someone, they would express their sympathy. I was not sure about my future. So I decided I would continue to Australia, and on my way there I would make up my mind about whether to continue sailing alone.

I really wanted to leave New Zealand immediately and put all this behind me, but this was not a good time to leave because it was typhoon season.

I needed something to do with my time. I worked all day long on the boat, trying to find jobs to keep me busy. New Zealand has some beautiful woods that are like teak. It is the same color and does not rot and will stand up to moist climates.

I decided to rebuild the interior of my boat. I had done a rush job while in the States just so I could get going on my cruise. I had planned to do it right sometime along my cruise. I bought plenty of wood and had it cut to the width I wanted and began cutting and fitting it to the bulkheads (walls) and overhead (ceiling). This kept me busy for a few weeks and kept my mind off the tragedy.

After I finished, I was proud of how lovely she looked with my kerosene lamps and the bronze sculpture I had made of a swordfish (Xiphias).

Charles saw what I had done and asked me if I would do the same on *Mintaka*. Why not, it was still typhoon season and I could not leave New Zealand yet.

I was nearly finished with *Mintaka* when there was a horrible storm. It rained ten inches in a matter of four hours. The river current was flowing very hard and suddenly I saw unmanned boats drifting down the current of the river. I figured they had been anchored and the anchors gave away. Then I saw the water was rising rapidly and my mooring lines were far underwater.

Suddenly, *Mintaka* floated past me as Charles yelled that I had his tiller and he was at the mercy of the river. Yes, I had removed the tiller to make room to store the wood for his interior. Then I realized it must be a flash flood and seconds later *Xiphias* tore away from its mooring poles and was also being carried down the river at a remarkable speed.

I started the engine, but I found I had little if any control. Fortunately, I was in the middle of the river so I just had to wait it out until I really had to do something. As the river entered the bay, where the water gets shallow, I realized I could throw my anchor overboard and *Xiphias* might come to a stop. I threw the anchor off the bow and let out a lot of chain as she continued moving with the current.

The anchor dragged for a while as I continued to put out more chain. Eventually, she came to a stop. Then I saw boats heading for me with no one aboard. I had to continuously fend off these boats, and then there was a huge tree that I could not get away from. I spent the night fending debris off the tree so it would not build up resistance and push harder against my boat.

Finally, the current eased and the tide began to drop. Then I realized, I was hard aground and beginning to lean over farther

and farther. I could see *Mintaka* not far from me. He was also aground in the shallow water.

The next day, at high tide, help arrived and they were able to pull all the boats that had gone aground into deeper water. Unfortunately, many boats had sunk, and others were a total loss.

Managing to pull my anchor chain loose from under the tree I began motoring towards *Mintaka*. After passing Charles his tiller I started motoring upriver.

I saw Keith and Angela's boat, *Kimimuana* on the rocks. This was the boat of my close New Zealand friend who had taken us to Auckland to fly back to the States.

When I got back to where I had been moored, I realized that this may not be the place I want to be. It had too many bad memories and the flash flood was the last straw. I would have lost my boat had I not been aboard.

I decided to return to Opua to anchor and plan for my sail to Australia. I had enough tragedy here and it was time to go somewhere else.

It was still typhoon season, but I did not give a damn at this point. I wanted to get away from all the reminders of what had happened. I knew I would miss the close friends I had made there. The bottom line is that New Zealanders are special, caring people.

Chapter 10
Australia

As I approach my destination in Queensland, Australia, I must survive a typhoon coming down the Coral Sea. I find work and learn many local customs that are different than mine. I learn the hard way about things to do and what not to do or say.

Ileft New Zealand for Australia. I was a bit concerned because it was still typhoon season, but it was rare for typhoons to ever go this far south. As I sailed toward Australia, I was still thinking about what had happened to Chris, and if there was anything I could have done to have prevented this tragedy? I wondered how Cindy was handling all this, with me not by her side. She must be suffering more than I. Now, I regretted not asking Cindy to return to *Xiphias* with me. I figured I would never see her again. She wanted me to come back and fit into society with her and Ashley. Yes, I had a choice, but I decided to follow my heart and keep sailing. I wanted to continue living my dream.

I was only a day's sail away from the Queensland coast when my radio announced a typhoon rapidly moving down the Coral Sea towards Brisbane, Queensland. Brisbane is where I had planned to enter Australia, but now I was concerned because this typhoon was now heading toward me. I had nowhere to run except to the open sea. It was the wrong season to leave New Zealand. I had not been thinking rationally at the time and I just wanted to get out. Now I regretted not waiting until the end of typhoon season.

By nightfall, the wind was up to 60 knots and the seas were breaking. Earlier, as the wind increased, I had dropped the sails and securely tied them down. Then I set my parachute anchor off the bow. This was like a parachute but only about eight feet in diameter.

It had a float to keep it near the surface. The objective was to prevent too much drift downwind and keep the bow to the wind and waves. I had practiced this procedure many times before I left California. The parachute was deployed without any problem. Now I just had to sit out the storm and hope and pray it did not get too much worse.

A huge wave passed under the boat and while I was in the trough, the wind would shift to my beam, turning it sideways to the waves. Then as soon as I was approaching the top of the next wave, *Xiphias* would heel over so the mast nearly touched the water and would suddenly turn and point into the wind. This went on all day and night. I dared not sleep so I sat inside the boat hoping and praying I would get through this OK. I thought I knew what I was doing. I had prepared and had been through similar storms. I would be OK.

By morning light, I could see that I was much closer to Moreton Island, which separated Moreton Bay from the passage into Brisbane and the open ocean. The waves were not as high and steep as yesterday. The wind had shifted and was now blowing me towards this island. The wind seemed to have dropped a little, but the waves were still high and rough.

I radioed to the Brisbane Harbor, asking for permission to enter the bay. They radioed back that the waves were too high for some of the shallow water and I could not enter Moreton Bay or Brisbane, it was too dangerous. They told me where there was an opening to a place called Mooloolaba, just north of me. It had a narrow pass but it was a safe place to keep my boat. They asked me to stay in radio contact until I arrived. Then they would send a Customs and Immigration official to meet me inside the harbor and check me into Australia.

It took me about an hour to get my parachute anchor aboard. I only raised the small, reefed, staysail, and started heading in the direction they had mentioned. Hours later I realized I was sailing downwind into a closed bay and there would be no turning back in these strong winds. I was worried about what would happen if I did not find the opening into the bay they mentioned.

I was about ready to radio Brisbane when I saw a fishing boat come out from behind some rocks. I thought this guy must be crazy to attempt to come out in these conditions, but just then it turned around and headed back in the way it came out.

As it entered, behind the rocks, a wave picked it up and pushed it sideways. I had no idea if it was damaged, or if it was safely inside the harbor. At least, I now knew where to enter the harbor.

It was blowing hard with horizontal rain that stung my face. When I approached the opening I started my engine and dropped my staysail. As I started to make my turn into the entrance, a wave picked me up and threw my stern near the rocks on the other side of the pass. I had my engine running at full throttle and managed to miss the rocks by, what seemed inches but it may have been feet. Either way, I was now inside the harbor and safe.

As soon as I was inside, I saw the powerboat that had come out and had shown me the way in. It was not a fishing boat but a government boat. He pointed for me to tie my boat between two poles then he waved for me to come to his boat.

In the pouring rain, I managed to tie *Xiphias'* stern to one of the poles, then the wind pushed me forward to the other. I had much difficulty tossing a line around the other pole because the wind kept carrying it downwind. I managed to let just enough line off my stern that my bowsprit was nearly touching the forward pole. I gave up trying to pass a line around the pole and made a big loop or lasso and threw it over the top of the pole. It took many tries, but I was finally safely moored.

I lowered my small rowing dinghy into the water and rowed ashore. Then I walked to his boat. He shook my hand and said, "G' day mate, Welcome to Australia." He had a strong accent; a bit like in New Zealand, but I noticed a slight difference. With a big grin on his face, he passed me a big shot of whiskey and said, "I called the Brisbane harbor patrol and told them you were safely here." "They are sending over the officials, and should be here in an hour."

He continued to tell me that he was a Harbor Pilot and he had heard my radio conversation with Brisbane. He continued, "Since you were only a 28-foot sailboat, I knew you only had one chance, so I decided to show you the way in."

I did my best to express my gratitude and thank him for his effort and the much-needed Scotch. This was my first experience with Australians, and I was more than impressed. I never expected I would get this kind of help anywhere in the world.

Soon the Customs officials arrived and cleared me. They explained that I was crazy to leave New Zealand and sail to Australia during the typhoon season. I tried to explain all that had happened in New Zealand and why I had to leave, knowing it was typhoon season. I told them I had spent the night at sea setting on my parachute anchor and how cooperative the authorities were to direct me to Mooloolaba. I thanked them so much for doing all this and even driving here to check me in. I was so grateful. Yes, I was most impressed with my introduction to Australians.

However, there was only one problem, I could not take a berth in a marina because *Pintle* was restricted to the boat. He could not go ashore under any circumstances. I could not afford a marina anyway.

I was exhausted and about half-drunk when I returned to my boat. I intended to move it upriver to the Mooloolaba Yacht Club in the next day or two.

The next morning, the harbor pilot, who had shown me the way in, called out for me to come over to his boat. He told me that the storm had driven a lot of boats onto the rocks at a place called Noosa Heads. He explained that he had to drive over there and look at the damage and make a report. He asked me if I wanted to go with him, which I gladly accepted.

It was a short drive to this point. There were a few boats that had gone aground and a few on the rocks. A lot of boats were damaged but there did not seem to be any loss of life. We returned to his harbor boat then soon I returned to my boat to get more sleep.

A few days later, I took a mooring between two poles directly opposite the Mooloolaba Yacht Club. They accepted me as a temporary member because I was a foreign cruiser. This is normal in most yacht clubs around the world, especially if you are a member of another Yacht Club.

Word spread rapidly about what had happened in New Zealand. I do not know how this word spread because I hadn't said anything to anyone except the harbor pilot and Customs officials. However, people were extremely friendly towards me and many expressed their sympathy.

I soon made friends with a young man who invited me to his home where he lived with his parents. He took me there in his car and would bring me back after dinner. I met his great family. I was accepted like a long-lost friend; I felt really welcomed.

My friend's mother told me she was cooking "chooks" and "snags" on the "barbie." I was surprised to see she was talking about chicken and king shrimp on the barbecue. They also told me a lot of other slang words I should know while I was in Australia that might keep me out of trouble; unfortunately, they forgot a few.

An "Aussie salute" was waving flies away from your face.

If something was "Fair Dinkum," it was the truth or real.

A "Pommy" was an Englishman. A "Yank' was an American.

A "Sheila" was a woman, any woman.

"Tea" was dinner.

If something went "Walkabout," it was lost.

"She'll be right mate," everything will be OK.

The list goes on and on and I cannot remember most of what I was told. I will have to learn as I go.

When it was time for dinner and we started eating, they explained to me that they eat with the fork, held upside down, in their left hand, and push food onto the fork with the knife, held in their right hand. This was like what we do back home only we move the fork to our right hand to put the food in our mouth.

Weeks later the young man said he had an older Holden car for sale really cheap, but I had to promise I would sell it back to him when I left. So now I had transportation. This is not as simple as it may sound because Australians drive on the other side of the road. It was difficult for me because when I left a parking space or parking lot, I immediately turned to my right, which was against the traffic. After

I realized it, I had to find a place to turn around. I had many close calls and I was "flicked" the middle finger several times.

I made a big sign and in bold letters, I wrote: **SORRY, I AM A YANK.** When I made this mistake, of accidentally driving on the wrong side of the road again, which was often, I showed this sign. I always got a smile and a wave.

One evening, while having a drink in the yacht club, a nice couple named Ginny and Fred, invited me to a fancy dress party. I figured this was a tuxedo type party, so I explained that I didn't have anything to wear. She laughed and said "No, fancy dress means a costume. You should come dressed as your favorite movie."

I accepted, but I was a bit worried because back home if I were to go to a costume party there would be some in a costume but many without. So, I was not sure what I should do. I had never seen any movies from Australia, and I was not sure how many American movies were shown here but I was sure everyone knew "Superman."

So, I found a shirt with the big Superman "S" in the middle. I dressed in nice clothes and a jacket that hid the big "S." I figured, like in America, if most were not dressed in a costume, I could keep my jacket closed or open to show I did try.

I bought a bottle of scotch (whiskey) and went to the party. When I knocked on the door, Ginny who had invited me said, "Roger, you did not dress for the party." "I should have told you that here in Australia you MUST dress, or you cannot join the party." At this point, I opened my jacket and she smiled and said, "Aww, Superman!"

Then she continued, "Guess who am I?" as she stepped back, she showed off her beautiful old wedding dress with a large bustle in the back. She had a fancy beer mug hanging around her neck with a hot dog or sausage sticking out the top of the mug. I told her I had no idea what her costume represented. She responded, "I am the bride of Frank-n-stein." I was impressed; then she led me in and began introducing me around.

We entered the kitchen where I saw some other clever costumes. I set my scotch on the table where they had set other bottles. As I passed a few guests, I heard behind me, "wouldn't you know it, the Yank came as Superman."

I had heard that some Australians were not big fans of Americans. This was leftover from the second world war because the American soldiers would make love to the Australian women while their boyfriends or husbands were away fighting the war. They were also upset because the Americans took all the credit for winning the war, not giving any credit to the men Australia lost fighting the Japanese in the Pacific.

Now, I felt awkward. Few people spoke to me. They had their own conversations and danced to the music. I felt out of place and began to drink my scotch. Slowly, it took effect and I began to feel better.

Ginny passed by and made a comment about Superman not dancing. I responded with "I love your costume and especially the 'fanny' in the back," meaning the large bustle. The party seemed to stop, and everyone was looking at me. Then a fat guy, dressed as Dracula, who set across the room from me said, "Hey Yank, do you know what you said to her?" I shrugged my shoulders and he continued, "You told her you like her pussy." Everyone laughed and I was now accepted. They explained to me that they thought it was hilarious that in America they had "fanny packs" while in Australia it was the term for a vagina.

When I returned to *Xiphias* and the yacht club, I began asking if there was any work available. Everyone said I should go to Sydney which was a big city and they are always looking for workmen in the different trades.

I decided to sail to Sydney to see what that big city was all about. The sail was rather easy with many anchorages where I could spend the night. I made it a point to visit some of the places where I anchored. It made my trip much more pleasurable and I got a chance to see things and places I would normally have missed.

Since I was sailing along the coast, I did not have to do much navigating because my chart would show me special landmarks, so I knew where I was for the whole trip.

As I entered the bay the first thing that caught my eye was the Sydney Opera House. I sailed right past it and admired its architecture. I was looking for a place I could safely anchor and go ashore but it was apparent this whole bay was for ships and not small sailboats.

I sailed back to a bay near the entrance and anchored. Then I took taxis and buses to see Sydney. I was looking for work because I was running out of money.

Sydney is a beautiful town and I really enjoyed it, but it was too big of a city for me and everything was a long distance from where I was anchored. I decided not to look for work and instead made the easy sail back to Mooloolaba.

When I returned, I took another mooring between polls at the Mooloolaba Yacht Club.

I planned to stay in Australia for about six months or longer because I had to find some work to earn some money. I only had a few thousand dollars when I left the States. While I was in Pago Pago, I had Cindy withdraw all my money from my teacher's retirement fund. When I was teaching, they did not take out Social Security, instead, they put a small percentage into a retirement fund they would match when I retired. If I quit teaching, I could withdraw what I had deposited. After teaching for 15 years, the total was about $10,000. I still had some money left but there had been some major expenses during our voyage, like flying back to California from New Zealand.

Living on a boat can be as expensive or inexpensive as you want it to be. Fortunately, I had lived frugally only spending money on diesel, rice, and some fruit and vegetables. I caught a lot of fish. I only really spent money in the cities.

By word of mouth, I found work in a metalworking company and my primary job was welding Roo Bars. In the States, we call them Bull Bars. These are a series of pipes welded together and installed on the front of the car to protect the car if you hit a big animal. There are many wild kangaroos in Australia, and it is common for someone to hit one while driving, so many of the cars had Roo Bars.

After working a few days, they asked me if I would like to order lunch. I had brought a sandwich, but I thought I would like to fit in more, so I said, "sure." Soon, a guy arrived and took our order. The others ordered hamburgers and I ordered a cheeseburger.

About 30 minutes later the guy returned with our orders. Mine was two hamburger buns with cheese in the middle. I told him I had ordered a cheeseburger and he told me it was a cheeseburger. If I wanted a hamburger with cheese, I should have said so. One of my fellow workers wanted to split half of his hamburger with half of my cheeseburger. I knew he just felt sorry for me, but I traded my half for his half. As I bit into the half hamburger, I discovered it had pineapple in it. I was surprised but it tasted good.

One afternoon, my boss said he would like to "shout" me a beer after work. So, we went to a pub and he bought two "stubbies" or glasses of beer. He then explained that when a person "shouts" you a beer, it is customary to buy him one back. I felt this was like in the States when you buy a round, but we did not have a name for it. After exchanging a few beers, a friend of his came in and my boss introduced us. His friend wanted to "shout" us a beer. Which meant he would buy three beers, one for each of us and one for himself. This meant that my boss and I, each had to "shout" him one back. So now I had already consumed our original two beers my boss and I had bought each other. Another beer his friend had bought us, and we had to buy a round each. That makes it about five beers in a short period of time. Australian beer is good but a bit stronger than what I was used to. I was getting drunk fast.

Then after another friend entered, it started all over again. When I returned to my car, I was drunk and found myself vomiting on the ground next to my car. Fortunately, I made it back to the yacht club and my boat safely, but I knew I should not have been driving. I went out to the boat and immediately passed out.

The next day, I told my boss what happened. He laughed and explained to me a simple solution. If I do not want to get involved in a "shout," I should order something more expensive than a beer. This was my solution for the future, and for me it worked perfectly the rest of the time I was in Australia.

After a few months, I found I could make more money working in construction. I got a job as a form carpenter who builds the forms for laying concrete. It was apparent that I did not know what I was doing but I knew how to use power saws and work with wood. The other workers told me what to do and I did exactly as I was told.

The boss told me that it was apparent that I did not know how to make concrete stairs but I was a hard worker, and a quick learner. I always showed up early, left late, and he did not have to pay any taxes or unemployment fees because I was working illegally. So, he was happy with my work.

I worked in form carpentry for another few months. Then the building we were working on was finished. The crew had to go into the interior to work on another building. I did not want to leave my boat and my cat, so I looked for other work.

There was a French cruiser who had started his own painting business and got lots of jobs painting new apartment buildings. He needed a lot of help and offered me more than I was earning as a form carpenter, so I started painting. That was not as easy as it sounds because I often had to stand on the outside of a wall, on an edge, many floors up, to paint the overhang or the underside of the balcony above. It was extremely dangerous, and I almost refused to do it. However, the Aussies were doing it without concern no matter what floor level.

I was not so brave so I brought a harness and some rope from my boat so I could tie one end to a doorknob or something and the other end to my harness. Fortunately, I never had to test if it worked or not. The Aussies certainly got a kick out of it.

Finally, I had earned enough money to continue cruising. I really did not want to continue alone, so I decided I would place an advertisement in the local Mooloolaba newspaper. Unfortunately, I did not get a single response. Then one day a writer from the paper

 came down to my boat and asked me if I had any response from my ad. I told her "no." Then she asked if she could take a photo and she would write a better ad for me.

The next day, I could not believe it, I was on the front page of the paper. The title was, "No takers for Paradise." I soon had many inquiries.

All my friends called me "Mr. Paradise." They meant it as a joke, and some gave me a pretty hard time but the write-up in the paper worked.

I met one couple that I liked, and they wanted to sail with me to the Solomon Islands. So, I agreed but when it was time to leave, the guy had family problems and could not go with us.

His girlfriend Michelle, however, still wanted to go with me. For some strange reason he was OK with this. I was totally surprised he would let her go alone with me. Michelle and I went on and became good, platonic friends.

I wanted to document this leg of my journey to the Solomon's but in those days video cameras were a new thing and sensitive to moist climates, so I bought a 16 mm camera and many rolls of film.

I finally made a film titled, " Melanesian Adventure by Roger Olson" (http://youtu.be/HpHYnsDNo9A). It is still available on YouTube, but the color is bad. The film I shot had to stay on the boat for months before I could have it developed. After developing the film it was OK, but then it sat for a long time in the humid climate and the whole thing turned dark. However, the story is interesting, and I think you would enjoy watching it. Especially if you read about our trip that follows.

Chapter 11
Melanesia

New Caledonia, Vanuatu, Banks Island, and the Solomon Islands. A local lady answers my ad and wants to sail with me to the Solomon Islands. This is where we learn more than expected about different cultures and customs.

*M*ichelle and I had a great, downwind sail to New Caledonia. We entered through the reef into the town of Noumea as I had the last time I was here. We spent some time anchoring in the same spot where I had anchored before where a river cascaded into the ocean. Perfect for doing laundry. We only spent a few weeks here then left for Vanuatu.

We found a group of small reef islands about a day's sail out of New Caledonia. The passage was narrow as was the anchorage. The land was flat so there was no protection from the wind, but the water was calm. We only spent one night and at first light, we left for Port Vila, Vanuatu.

Our sail was uneventful. We arrived late one afternoon and spent at least a week in Port Vila before we left for Tanna Island which has a huge bay for anchoring and a live volcano where one could walk to the top.

We entered the bay, but it was much shallower than we figured so we had to anchor out in the middle which was a long row to shore.

We went ashore the next morning, and we saw a small village with grass houses, which is common throughout the South Pacific. We met a young man hunting with a bow and arrow along a dirt road, so we knew there were cars on the island and a bigger village somewhere, but we had no desire to go into town. We only wanted to see the volcano.

He and his younger brother agreed to take us to the crest of the volcano where we could stand on the edge and look straight down into the bubbling lava. It was almost straight down, and our guide gestured that it was dangerous to stand too close, but we remained where we were, mesmerized by the sight.

Then it started bubbling stronger. The next thing we knew, it blew up and the sky was full of smoke and lava. Fortunately, our guide had taken us to the windward side so everything was blowing away from us. We spent several hours on this edge because we realized  that there are few if any places in the world where one can stand on the edge of a live volcano and peer down into the active center.

Vanuatu, which used to be called the New Hebrides, was famous for the village where the natives had built a high tower out of wood and the men tied vines at the top that would nearly reach the ground. Then they would climb to the top, tie one end of the vine to their ankles, and jump, headfirst, like bungy-jumping. Unfortunately, they were not jumping when we were there. But we did get a chance to see the tower. We spoke to the people and learned that this custom had been practiced for more years than they could remember. Its objective was to show their sincerity to their God of how important it was to have a good harvest.

Next, we visited an island occupied by large and small Nambas. These native men wore nothing to cover their privates, except for the tip of a dried gourd over their penis. This gourd is tied around their waist and their testicles hang loose.

They were separated into two villages: the Big Nambas and the Small Nambas. (Large gourds or small gourds to cover their penis's.)

The authorities discouraged us from visiting because these natives were not exposed to developed cultures and they were unpredictable. We decided to anchor off the island, but were still able to see some of them standing onshore.

After leaving the many primitive islands we continued to the Banks islands of Vanuatu. This is near where Vanuatu separates from the Solomon Islands.

We found a river cascading down into a beautiful bay. Another perfect place to anchor, get some rest and do some laundry.

I tried snorkeling to see if I could spear some fish for dinner while Michelle washed clothes. There were few fish to be found and it was hard to see because the top 6 to 7 inches was fresh water that was not clear but as soon as I got my face mask below this fresh water, the water was crystal clear.

Later that afternoon, we saw a native with a long spear standing on a rock on a point at the end of the bay. It was apparent he was hoping to spear a fish. So, there must have been some fish in these waters.

We saw his wife making a fire, so we went over to say hello. They could not speak any English, as was the case in most of the places we visited, but sign language always worked well. She began to draw a crocodile in the sand. I thought she was trying to sell us some crocodile meat or skin, so I shrugged and shook my head "no." Little did I know what she was trying to tell us was that the bay had a large, man-eating crocodile in it and I should not be diving in the bay.

After a few days of catching up on our rest, we were preparing to raise the anchor when another larger sailboat from Australia came into the anchorage. We waved at the guys and took off for the Santa Cruz Islands.

The next day, we heard on the radio that the other boat was asking for help because one of their crew had been taken by a large crocodile and they did not know where he was. Now I understood what the women were trying to tell me and how lucky I was not to have been taken by that crocodile.

We entered the bay of the Santa Cruz Islands where we officially checked into the Solomon Islands. We spent a few days there and heard there was a small group of islands called the Reef Islands that was in the opposite direction to the rest of the Solomon's and no one ever went there. We decided to make the two to three-day sail to check it out.

We were about 12 hours from the first island when we saw a young man in a dugout canoe that was full of water. The seas were rough and no matter how much he tried to bail out the water, more water would enter. Since the dugout canoe was just a tree log with the center dug out, it would not sink but he was a long way from land. We sailed over to him and pulled him aboard. We tried to pull his dugout on board, but it was far too heavy. We managed to get a line tied to it and towed it behind us.

Hours later, he showed us the pass into the Reef Islands, but it looked shallow and I was afraid he did not understand that our boat was much deeper than a dugout canoe.

It was a narrow passage but just deep enough for our draft. Inside the pass, it got shallow rapidly. Before we could set anchor, he dove overboard, climbed into his canoe, and paddled ashore with

his boat still full of water. Fortunately, the anchorage was calm. Later that afternoon we went ashore and saw it was a relatively large village with grass houses which had curtains for doors.

We walked for a distance and did not see a single person. After over an hour the guy we had helped, came out yelling something behind him. Slowly people began to show themselves. It looked like we were the first, or it had been many years since they had seen a white person. They would touch our nose and peer up and down our bodies. They always stared into my blue eyes. They were not overly friendly, unlike the other islands we had visited after leaving Australia, and they were more curious, but we did not feel the least bit threatened.

We decided to anchor farther away from the town so we found a little island that we could anchor near and still have only a short row to the village.

We spent nearly a week on the boat only spending brief times ashore. Then it was time to continue our cruise through the Solomon Islands. We found there were lots

of islands with a huge channel between most of them.

We decided to work our way to San Cristobal Island and then go to the southern tip of Guadalcanal. When we were ready, we crossed over to Auki on Malaita Island. Then we would sail down the Longa Longa lagoon and cross back to Guadalcanal where the capital, Honiara was located.

As we visited these islands, we discovered there were talented wood carvers who used mother of pearl seashells, cut and embedded into pieces of wood. These were designed like the tattoos they wore. We ended up buying a lot of these carvings. Well, not actually buying but trading items for them.

We loved all the islands and villages we visited. Our favorite was the islands in the Malaita group because they had a beautiful channel and we could anchor anywhere we wanted, with permission from the Chief of the village. This was the custom throughout the South Pacific.

When we entered an anchorage where we wanted to anchor, we were always visited by children in dugout canoes. Some had outriggers on the sides that prevented them from capsizing but these were hard on our boat. They always came alongside our boat and the heavy, hard dugout canoes left scratches and stains on the side of our boat. They would stand up in their dugouts and investigate our windows or portholes. This would go on day and night.

Through sign language and a bit of pidgin English, we asked them who was their leader by pointing a finger at all of them, then put one finger up in the air and shrug like asking a question. They would always point to one boy who was probably the chief's son. We would invite only him aboard, and we would try to explain that we wanted him to keep the other canoes away from our boat.

This always worked. Then we would ask him if we could anchor where we were. If not, he would show us where we should go. We would tow his canoe behind us and go where he suggested. We did not always accept his choice, but we always found a safe anchorage that satisfied everyone.

Several times I would find a place we liked, and the boy would start to laugh and suggest we don't anchor there. Later, we discovered it was where the villagers did their defecation.

After we anchored, somewhere else, we would ask the boy to take a small gift to the village chief. Sometimes it would be a spool of fishing line or a big box of matches or fishing lures, etc.

We asked the boy to ask the chief if we could come ashore to visit his village. Within an hour the boy would return and nod his head that it was OK to go ashore.

We were always welcomed by the villagers. Often a person who spoke a little English would show us around the village and tell us to keep away from the place where they all would defecate. We were always followed by most of the villagers who would stare at us and touch our skin or nose. They were always taken aback by our eyes. Many times, the children would come to the shoreline to see us off.

We learned that in the outer islands they did not use money as we know it, but instead, they would gather different colored seashells. They would break them into small pieces then use a small hand drill that worked by turning a handle on the side that turned the drill

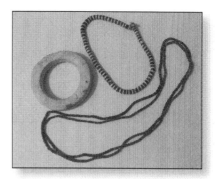

and this would make a small hole through the shell.

These pieces were then threaded on a line through the hole in the center. Then they would use a rock with a groove to grind the line of small pieces into round, small discs. Depending on the colors, a strand of these shells had value. Some were more valuable than others and they were used to trade for goods, food, brides, etc.

The large white ring is a white stone that they used for money before they started using shell money. These stone rings are rare and are no longer made. They have considerable value in western culture because of their history.

After about two months in these islands, we headed to Gizo where Michelle would fly back to Australia. We stopped at the Russell Islands then we went on to the New Georgia group. Here we entered

the beautiful Marovo Lagoon that was miles and miles long and well-protected by a barrier reef.

We stopped at one small island and met a family from Australia who were missionaries trying their best to convert the locals to Christianity. They told us about a sacred burial ground on the top of this mountain where the headhunters left their trophies. Their young son agreed to show us the way.

It was a steep, difficult climb. When we arrived at this small cave, our butts were hanging over a steep cliff as we peered inside to see a huge stack of skulls. Too many to count from where we stood.

From there we continued up the lagoon and anchored at various islands. We anchored off one small village called Telina. We met a very friendly family. The head of this family was also a woodcarver and he played the "Baboos" which were bamboos.

These were various lengths of hollow bamboos set one on top of the other. He would hit the ends with a thong, and it made a sound similar to a drum. He was talented, to say the least. His brother would play the guitar while their wives and children sang.

I saw a few samples of his wood carvings and he was undoubtedly the best I had seen. I asked him to carve one for me. He found some black ebony wood and said he would carve fish out of it with his brother spear fishing. In exchange, I would give him a kerosene lantern with two extra mantels.

After a week or so, we had to get on to Gizo, so I made radio contact with a boat that I knew was about a week behind us. I asked them if they would bring our carving with them and we would pick it up later. So, reluctantly, I gave John his lantern and he would give my carving to my friends when they arrived.

This went perfectly. Our friends gave me the carving when we met at Bougainville Island in Papua New Guinea.

The carving was about 20" tall and 12" wide at the base. There was not a single space on the whole piece that did not have some kind of sea life perfectly carved into it. It was full of fish, sharks, lobsters, turtles, crabs, etc. and on the top was a full-length person swimming to the surface with a speared fish in his hand. It was far better than I had dreamed it would be.

After we raised anchor, we continued our sail to the Blackett Strait. This is where there was a deserted World War II Japanese airbase named Munda. They would cover the runway with bent palm trees to hide it until it was needed to attack or defend against the Americans or Australians.

We continued to the end of the straits where we anchored at Anohe Bay. Here we found five large Japanese guns aimed out to sea. Apparently, these guns were to protect the airbase from enemy ships. I was amazed at how they were in such good shape. There were still a lot of things from the war laying around, like old shell casings. The locals took the powder out of them and used it in coconut shells as a bomb to kill fish.

We spent a week there looking around and taking our dinghy up the channel to see more things from the war. Then it was time to get my friend to Gizo so she could be home for Christmas. We headed off at first light in a soft breeze for Gizo.

Just before reaching Gizo, we passed Kasolo Island. Sometimes it is referred to as Kennedy Island because this is where John F. Kennedy swam to when his PT 109 was rammed by a Japanese destroyer during World War II. Two sailors died in the incident. Later, John F. Kennedy and what was left of his crew, swam to Olasana Island which was bigger and had coconuts to eat and drink.

We sailed on to Gizo where we spent several days before Michelle had to return to Australia. It was a sad goodbye because we had become good, "platonic" friends. Not that I did not try but she told me she was off-limits. I respected her wishes and thus our friendship flourished. It was a sad departure.

Alone, I left to sail to Papua New Guinea.

Chapter 12
Papua New Guinea and the Bougainville Copper Mine

Bougainville Copper Mine, Papua New Guinea: *The second largest, open pit, copper mine in the world that is run by Australia. I learn a lot about the various native Papua New Guinea customs. I catch malaria. I return home to testify for Jerry Whitworth and he tells me his side of the story about spying for John Walker (Family of Spies). After I return to Bougainville, I hear my brother is dying so I return home to be with him. While there, I get a message that the company is being invaded by a local revolutionary army and they are forced to close the copper mine. I must get my boat out while I can, so I must leave my brother and return to Bougainville to get my boat to the Solomon Islands and safety. I return home for my brother's passing.*

Now, I had to continue alone to the Treasury Islands where I spent nearly a week visiting some more World War II sights before I continued to Bougainville Island in Papua New Guinea. I had heard there was a large Australian copper mine on this island, and I might be able to find some work.

I entered Kieta Bay and saw a bunch of small sailboats moored in one area. I anchored in deep water and went ashore. There was a small grass-roofed open building with an open bar and no one around. I walked around and finally found a local who was taking care of the place. He told me it was the Kieta Yacht Club. I returned to *Xiphias* and waited until the evening when people started to arrive. It was a weekday so there were only about eight people who arrived, all Australians who worked for the Bougainville Copper Mine. I introduced myself and was welcomed by buying (shouting) me drinks and asking me about my travels.

I learned that the moored sailboats were all small McGregors that were brought over from the States on their company ship. They were trying, with the help of some hired locals, to build a concrete dock out into deeper water so they could load and unload supplies and guests on their small boats without having to row everything out in a small dinghy.

It was apparent that the people that were attempting to build this dock did not know what they were doing when it came to pouring the concrete. Also, they could only work on it during the weekends when they were not working in the mine.

Since I had worked as a form carpenter in Australia and I had nothing else to do, I volunteered to help. While they were at work during the week, I would work on their dock. On the weekends they were impressed by how much I had accomplished. After a few weeks, one of the local contractors offered me a supervisor's job for his crew who were all natives and spoke only Pidgin English.

This was my first experience with native workmen in Papua New Guinea. I had to learn "Pisin Wontok" (Pidgin English) to communicate. English is the national language in Papua New Guinea, but there are over 800 dialects or one language per village, so the villagers listen to our English and mix it with their dialect and come up with something that resembles English. It was not too difficult to learn because they wrote it as they heard it. An example was if I wanted a workman to "climb up into the truck," they heard "calupin long truk," one language, "Wontok."

The contractor I worked for repaired the homes that the copper mine furnished for all their employees. I quickly learned that these natives were from all over Papua New Guinea and were not very skilled workmen. They did not seem to think things through before they did them.

I asked one guy to put a sliding bolt lock on a bathroom door so the user would have privacy. He did a good job, but he put the lock on the outside of the door. Another had installed a new entrance door that had about a 3-inch gap on the top. I told him to replace the door with one that fit. When I returned the space at the top was gone but now it was on the bottom of the door. There are too many stories to tell but it was a most interesting experience.

My visa was soon to expire, and my boss had not submitted it for a work permit. I was upset with him and I put the word out that I was looking for work at the copper mine. I heard there was an opening for a position as "Senior Production Control Officer" in the Town's Department located in the town of Arawa, on the coast.

I knew the superintendent of the Town's Department because he was rebuilding a large sailboat that was sitting in his front yard. He gave me the job immediately. The company flew me to Australia where they got my passport stamped with a two-year, renewable work permit. I also signed a contract to work for the copper mine for these two years. I returned to Bougainville after a few days and immediately began working.

The copper mine, which was a huge open pit, was the world's second-largest. There were three major locations on Bougainville that belonged to the mine. The town of Panguna is where the huge open-pit mine was located. It was on top of a mountain, a long uphill drive from the larger town of Arawa on the coast, where most of the employees lived. Then there was the port of Loloho where the company had its own ships that traveled to various countries for supplies and to unload their copper and gold.

Since the company was on this island, they had to provide housing for every employee. If you were in a higher status with a family, you would get a nice two-story home. If you were more of a laborer, you got a small two-bedroom home. But if you were single, you got a small apartment with one bedroom. This is what they gave me. So, I moved off the boat and into my apartment.

My job was to check the homes when people left to make sure they left them in as good a condition as they were in when they moved in. There was a woman who went with me to inspect the homes in case there were no men around.

Almost everyone who worked for the mine was either educated Australians or local Papua New Guineans from all over the country. My second in charge was from the island of New Ireland, a volcanic island not far from Bougainville. He had a photographic memory and could tell me the names of each family who lived in any of the hundreds of homes in the town of Arawa where we had our offices.

I became good friends with a lot of the people who worked for the mine and some that were contractors. My superintendent who had the sailboat in his front yard often asked my opinion about boat projects. I ended up helping him a lot in my free time and we became the best of friends. Unfortunately, he had a heart problem and had to return to Australia for surgery periodically. After my second year, he died during surgery in Australia. His superintendent job became available, so I applied and immediately got it. I was now in charge of all the workmen and the housing department.

I had a crew of all the different trades: cabinet makers, carpenters, electricians, and plumbers, etc. If there was any work to be done on any of the many homes in Arawa, my men would do it. They were certainly more qualified than the men who worked for the local contractors. However, they did not have any kind of building codes or knowledge on how to do things the right way. So as Superintendent of the Town's Department, I wrote a long, detailed building code for the men to follow. It took a lot of time and study but it worked great.

Then I got malaria. I was taking a medication named Maloprim that was supposed to prevent one from getting malaria. I was later told that it will not prevent Malaria, but it will reduce the symptoms. I was miserable for months. I felt horrible all the time but much worse when I would get a sudden fever and the shakes. I went to the hospital many times to take blood tests, but it always came back negative. I had an extremely high white blood cell count, but no Malaria parasites were found. I lived with it, not knowing what it was.

Then once, while eating lunch with my boss, I started getting the shakes and a fever. This happened once or twice a day but only lasted for about half an hour. He told me to go to the hospital immediately. He called the hospital to expect me. They were waiting with a syringe in hand and took my blood. Yes, I had malaria.

Apparently, the malaria parasite lives in the liver and come out to feed on the blood cells. This is when the person starts the shakes and gets a high fever because all the white blood cells begin to attack the parasite. The only real way to find out if someone has malaria is to take their blood during a high fever and the shakes.

I was given a cure that had to be closely monitored because if I accidentally took too much, it could kill me. After less than a month I was back to normal. However, it returned, and I had to repeat the medication. To this day, I am not permitted to give blood.

Short break to discuss my friend, Jerry Whitworth.

One night I was awakened by a phone call from my brother. He told me that my friend, Jerry Whitworth had called him and asked him to call and tell me that he may be arrested for spying with a friend who was a warrant officer in the Navy. Both were radiomen who served on different ships. I could not believe it because Jerry and I had no secrets and he had never mentioned this.

I remembered, recently, seeing on the local military television (the only English TV station we got on Bougainville), the news about a guy in the Navy named John Walker who had been arrested for selling military secret codes to the Russians. His name was similar to the name of Jerry's friend, who I had met but we called him by the name of the scotch we all drink, Johnny Walker and he had hair. This guy on TV was bald. I then realized this was the same guy, but his name was John, not Johnny and he always wore a toupee when I saw him.

I had met this guy several times through Jerry. Jerry seemed to like him, but he seemed arrogant to me and I did not feel comfortable around him. I cannot explain why, but some people affect me that way. I kind of felt he was jealous of my friendship with Jerry. I only visited his home once to attend a party he was giving. I was surprised how well he lived being a warrant officer in the Navy. He lived alone but Jerry told me he had a wife who lived back east. He was a bit of a braggart about some of the things he owned. Once I asked him how he earned so much money and he told me it was because he was a "spy." I figured it was his way of joking, but apparently not.

A few weeks after the call from my brother, while at work, I got a call from the FBI and they wanted to come to Bougainville Copper Mine to talk to me. I met with them several times. Apparently, my name came up a lot when talking to Jerry's friends and they had listened to all the cassette tapes I had sent Jerry.

This was the way I communicated with my parents, brother, and Jerry. It was much easier to talk on a small cassette tape than to write a long letter. The FBI was concerned about a comment I had made to Jerry thanking him for the money he had sent for my birthday and what I had bought with it. They were concerned that I had been laundering money for him. I gave them my passport so they could check banks in every country I had visited to see if I had opened an account, which I had not.

I was required to fly back to San Francisco to testify in Jerry's defense. Unbeknown to me, at the time, I had malaria. I was in a bit of a daze when I appeared in court, but it did not affect my testimony. Afterward, I went to a medical clinic. They did a blood test and found nothing. I was feeling off all the time and when I got the fever and shakes, I was miserable and thought I might die.

I was permitted to visit Jerry in jail, and he told me the story of how his warrant officer friend, had told him he would be helping the Israelis with a few coded items. Both Jerry and I were pro-Israel, so this did not surprise me much. Apparently, he had started doing this, not for the money but to help Israel. Then after a year or more, he learned that his friend was lying and instead was selling the information to the Russians. Jerry was pissed off and told him he wanted no part of it. His friend's response was that the Russians would kill Jerry and/or his wife.

Jerry told me he did not know what to do because he believed it might be true about the Russians killing him or his wife. He decided to put an ad in the classified section of the San Francisco Examiner, using an alias name. The ad was addressed to the FBI and said that he had information on a spy, and he would tell them everything for immunity. They did not respond. Jerry felt he had no other choice but to continue until his time was up in the Navy, then he would retire. This would get him away from his so-called "friend" and his spying.

The only reason they caught Jerry's friend was that he tried to recruit his own daughter who was in the Army. She refused to help him. A few years later, she and her husband had a son. They later divorced and the ex-husband took their son without telling her. She went to her father to ask for his help, but he told her she was better off without a child. Her father's comment was so upsetting she went to her mother, told her about her father's response, and explained what he had asked her to do while she was in the Army. This greatly upset his wife. She knew about his spying for years. She had previously called the Boston FBI and told them about her husband's espionage. Unfortunately, she was drunk at the time she made the call, so it was ignored by the FBI as a crank call.

The spy's wife's landlord had a good friend who was an FBI agent. She told her landlord everything and asked him to speak to his FBI friend. Soon the FBI interviewed his wife and daughter to hear their stories. Then the FBI put a tail on John.

Several weeks later they caught him making a drop. He got a lesser sentence by telling the FBI who else was helping or working with him. This included his brother and his son. It also included Jerry. Unfortunately, his wife regretted what she had done because she had no idea that he had involved their son in his espionage ring. He had tried to get the whole family to work with him but only his daughter had rejected his offer.

They made a movie about him and several books were written about how this spy had involved his family in his spy ring (Family of Spies, Inside the John Walker Spy Ring by Pete Earley).

John Walker passed away in jail at the age of 77. Poor Jerry is still in prison for trying to help the Israelis and may remain there for the rest of his life. He was my best friend, like a brother. He did it for the Israelis, not the money. I still communicate with him on a regular basis.

I visited him while he was in Leavenworth and several times after he was transferred to Atwater, California.

This does not infer that I approved of what he did. Simply, we were like brothers and I understand he had made a mistake. We all have, but that does not change who he was and is to me, my brother.

My last visit with Jerry was with my wife. She had heard me speak of Jerry so much, she wanted to meet him.

To this day, there are people who believe I was involved in this spy ring because Jerry and I were so close.

The news media went to my parents' house in Fresno, California, and asked them what they thought about their son being a spy. My parents knew it was untrue and let the news media have it. They even got a lawyer to try to get a lawsuit against the TV station but the lawyer said it was difficult to sue them and they let it go.

Let me assure you I was not, nor could I have been involved but there will always be some who believe I was.

Back to Bougainville Copper Mine.

After a few years, it became apparent that the Bougainville Copper Mine was spending a lot of money on the homes and salaries for these workmen. My manager and I decided we could save money if we let our workers start their own contract business with the promise that we would use them as our contractors. We only kept the supervisors of each trade to oversee the work.

Of course, the workers would have to move out of the small houses the company provided, or they could pay a small amount of rent. This worked out well and everyone was happy. They earned more money as contractors than they did working for the company. The company got far more work done for less money and time.

I was paid well at the copper mine, but they only wanted to pay us cash equal to the same amount of cash as the locals got paid or about 25% of our actual salary. The rest they would deposit in any bank of our choice anywhere in the world. This was done because they did not want it to appear the Australians were earning more money than the locals.

I did file my income taxes but when you earn your money while working overseas one only has to pay taxes on what they earn after they have paid their local taxes where they work and anything over $70,000. Unfortunately, I never exceeded that amount, but it was a lot of money back in those days and all my living expenses were paid for by the company.

I saved a lot of money during my years working at the mine and I made many great friends. I am still in contact with some after over 30 years.

I wanted to learn as much as I could about the way the locals lived because Papua New Guinea is a very primitive country. They practiced cannibalism only a few years before I arrived. To learn more about them, I would take a group of my employees sailing on the weekend and after they had a few beers, I would ask them questions about their village and customs.

No one wanted to talk about it for some reason. After a few trips, one of my senior employees told me that there was a lot of tribal warfare between villages and no one wanted to reveal any special customs that might help the other villages use against them.

Tribal warfare was real. I spoke to several missionaries who told me similar stories on how the natives would come to their service then go to war immediately afterward. We also would, on occasion, find a body part in a field. Apparently, there was a fight and they all carry machetes for just such a situation.

My friend told me to take only "Wontoks" (one talk or one dialect language) from one village and I could learn anything I wanted to know.

Wow did that work. I learned that some villages still ate their village chief when he died. Each village had a man of magic (puripuri man) that had the power to put curses on people.

In many villages, if a person dies for some unknown reason like suddenly getting ill and progressively getting worse, they suspected it was from a magic curse put on the ill person by a "puripuri man." However, they could not be sure so they would place his spear on the floor next to the body. For 24 hours no one could enter the home, which was a grass house with a curtain door. Then only the chief and the puripuri man could enter. If the spear had not moved its position, then the person died of natural causes. However, if the spear had moved even a few inches, then he was killed by a curse placed on him by a puripuri man of another village.

If the spear had moved, they would pick up the spear and rest it in the palm of their hands and the spear would begin to move. They would only support the spear as it moved on its own. The spear would lead them to a grass house with a curtain door. The chief would call out for the man to come out. Soon as he opened the curtain, the spear would thrust itself into the chest of the man.

I asked the man telling me the story if the man who was going to die ever said he did not do it. He explained to me that the man would always say he didn't do it but the spear knows the truth because the spear was thrust into the man's chest by its own power, without the help of the men holding the spear.

All the others from the same village who were on my boat would agree with him. This made me think of our "Ouija" or "Spirit Board."

One of my close friends was a doctor who did medical missionary work in impoverished places around the world. He asked me if I would sail him and a couple of nurses out to an island about a hundred miles from Bougainville Island. He said he had heard they needed some medical care.

I agreed and we took off early one morning and arrived late the next day. It was too late to attempt to enter the pass in the reef because the sun was low and in front of us and we could not see any dangers under the surface in that light. The best time to enter these lagoons is when the sun is behind or overhead. We sailed around to the lee side of the island, so we were protected from the waves and the wind.

That evening we were all sitting in the cockpit of *Xiphias* and I asked him what he thought about the puripuri magic. He smiled and said he really did not know how to explain it but he had many cases where a person was brought to the hospital who did not respond to medication but their puripuri man cured them. One such case he mentioned, was of a man who had his vital organs slowly failing. They attempted to treat him without any positive results. It was apparent the person would die.

The family asked if they could bring in their own puripuri man and the doctor said he had nothing to lose so why not. Then, to his surprise, a day or two later, the person who was going to die, suddenly started to improve rapidly.

We talked about this and we concluded that if the human body wants to heal itself, it has the power to do so. The problem was how to convince the body to cure itself. If a person strongly believes that a puripuri man has the power, he might believe strongly enough, that he cures himself. Then, of course, there is the belief that the ill man had a curse on him and the puripuri man removed the curse. Miracles do happen. It may be God who does it. Who knows?

Since the Bougainville Copper Mine hired men from all over Papua New Guinea, there were many different "wontoks" that had their own customs and occasions they celebrated. Normally, it was private and only "wontoks" could attend. It could be dangerous for an outsider to witness these ceremonies. Fortunately, I was often invited because some of the natives worked for me.

Some of these events were frightening because of their dress and actions. We would often see a local walking around the area in this type of dress during a normal day, so we knew what tribe they were from and he wanted all to know because of a possible tribal war.

Bougainville was a volcanic island with several volcanoes, one of which was highly active. We had many earthquakes and just learned to accept them. In fact, most of the homes were built on steel stilts so when an earthquake hit, the steel supports took most of the shaking.

A good friend of mine was a seismologist. He would set equipment on the side of the volcano to monitor the movement and how often it occurred. He had to go up there in a helicopter to remove the data and replace it with a new tape about every few months.

One day he was going up to exchange the tape and he asked me if I would like to join him. Unfortunately, the helicopter pilot was in Australia, so we had to use his assistant who came over to temporarily replace him.

We flew over the volcano and dropped my friend on the side of the volcano. The arrangement was that the helicopter pilot would come back and pick him up in about half an hour, so we flew around the volcano and I had a chance to take a few photos.

After picking up my friend, the pilot said he saw a big sinkhole he wanted to investigate. This sinkhole has huge. You could fit at least ten football fields inside it.

As we approached, it was apparent that there was a huge cave at the bottom with a river running through it. The pilot flew down to take a closer look and the entrance was huge. He decided he would like to fly into the cave for only a short time.

He admitted he had never flown a helicopter inside a cave before and it looked big enough that he could do it without any problem. My friend and I were excited but also worried. This pilot had never done it before!

We were fully inside the cave when the pilot says, "problem." He immediately backed the helicopter out of the cave and explains to us that the blades push air down to keep the helicopter in the air. Unfortunately, this force of air has nowhere to go but up the sides of the cave and push down on us from the top. He had to keep increasing the pitch of the blades to keep us in the air. In a short time, we would be in the rapids of the river below. We were all happy to get back to the Arawa airport.

Soon as I went back to work, I was told that an Australian friend of mine had to go back to Australia because of a local emergency. Apparently, he had hit and killed a pig while driving. Pigs are sacred in some villages. He was immediately attacked by some locals, so he drove directly to the police station for protection. The police immediately took him to the company airport and sent him home, never to return.

Once, on a Saturday, my men were watching American basketball on television. They were all local Papua New Guineans but from a different island or parts of the country. I heard several of them use the term "that stupid nigger." I was almost in shock. I asked them what they meant by calling a person of color, (these men were all black) a nigger. I explained that it was a negative term that should not be used. Their response was that it was a common term used for black Americans who are originally from Africa. I asked them if it would apply to them. They said no, they were Papua New Guineans.

I explained that it would be best not to use that term. It was a word that is negative like a curse word. I did not mention that it could be applied to them if they were in the States.

My plumbing foreman decided he wanted to go visit the United States. He had a lot of custom tattoos on his face, so I figured he might get by without a problem. When he returned, we all met on my boat, drinking beer as he told us about his trip. The first thing he said, reluctantly, was that they called him a nigger. That the term applies to anyone of dark color. He told them he was from Papua New Guinea but that did not matter.

Then he told us about going to the bar in his hotel where he met this lovely white girl. After a few drinks, apparently, she wanted to go to his room. He explained how she kissed with her tongue and groped him. He found this extremely exciting until she dropped her pants and to his extreme surprise she had a penis. Everyone burst out laughing and asked him what he did when he saw it was not a woman? His response was, "I told it to get out of my room." Then after a few moments passed, he said, "It was really sexy, and I thought about what I had done, so I called it back into my room." At that point, we had tears running down our faces from laughing so hard.

The huge open-pit mine took up a lot of the land that had originally belonged to the people. So, at the request of the copper mine, the Papua New Guinea government bought the land from the people so the mine could start digging their open pit.

As the mine grew, more and more families were displaced. Over the years, one family who sold their property earlier learned that the family who recently sold their land had gotten more money. This led to a lot of protests. The mine tried to explain to them that their government and not the mine was responsible for how much anyone got paid for their land, .

As time passed, there was more hate toward the mine, and eventually, they organized the "Bougainville Revolutionary Army (BRA)" who intended to close the mine. It started by blowing up the electrical power towers that fed electricity from Loloho on the coast, up the mountain to the mine. The refinery and the town of Panguna could not function without electricity. The Papua New Guinea government sent over some military troops to control the BRA. This gave the company the time to replace the electrical towers that had been blown up. Then it got worse when the BRA started shooting at the company buses that took employees up the mountain to work in the mine.

This caused the Papua New Guinea Military to set up a base in Arawa. The war got worse and the military reportedly molested some of the women on the island. It was beginning to get so bad no one wanted to leave their homes to go to work or when they had time off. The BRA attacked the military base one night, killing many of the soldiers.

About this time, I got a phone call from my brother in California, telling me that he had bone cancer and may only have a few months to live.

I had an Australian friend who loved cats, so he agreed to live in my place to look after "Pintle." I took the first company flight back to Australia and the first flight I could get to my brother's place in California. It was sad what I saw when I arrived. My brother had lost a lot of weight and was taking radiation regularly that made him look extremely sick.

The cancer had begun in his bladder and was not detected even though he had blood in his urine. The cancer moved to his prostate. He had both his bladder and prostate removed and thought he was OK. Then he had pain in his right arm, just below the shoulder. This revealed he had bone cancer and did not have much more time to live. They pinned the cancer-ridden bone in his arm so he could function. During my time with him, we often spoke about the future and his attitude about dying.

I was mad at him for not trying to beat it by stopping his smoking and trying other holistic cures. I wanted him to believe he could cure himself. These discussions often ended up in a heated argument.

The bottom line is that I was having great difficulty accepting the fact that my brother was going to die in his early 50's. I now realize that he knew his cancer had progressed too far, so he just wanted to enjoy the time he had left and not argue with his younger brother.

Then I got a phone call from a female friend of mine who ran the local travel agency in Arawa. She told me the mine was closing and there was only one more company plane flying from Australia to Bougainville Island. She had booked me on this last flight which left Australia in three days.

She also booked my flight from San Francisco to Australia. I had to get my boat out of Bougainville, or I would lose it. I explained my situation to my brother and promised I would be back as soon as I possibly could.

I caught the first flight back to Australia and managed to catch the last flight into Arawa. Two days after I arrived, the BRA blew up the landing field so no plane could leave or arrive.

Fortunately, most everyone had already left, leaving all the mining equipment, worth billions of dollars, and all the company homes vacant. I did not have much time. I had to get my boat out of there as soon as possible.

My lady friend from the tour agency could not fly out now that there was no airport so she wanted to go with me to the Solomon Islands where we could leave the boat and both fly home. We headed down to my boat, which was moored in front of the Kieta Yacht Club. There were still a few boats there that had been abandoned.

The problem was, we had no food or supplies so I motored *Xiphias* to the Loloho Pier. There was a storage building where ships stored the goods they brought in from Australia and other countries. There was one guy there who gave us anything we wanted. He asked us if we had room and I explained that it was only a 28-foot boat, but he could go with us to the Solomon Islands if he wanted. He said that before we had arrived, he was planning to drive to the other end of the island the next day. Then he would catch a commercial boat going to Port Moresby, the capital of Papua New Guinea. He decided to stay with that plan instead of going with us.

As we were loading *Xiphias*, shots rang out close by so we left with what we had on the boat, leaving the rest on the pier. As we headed away from land, we could see and hear shots being fired. We were not sure if they were meant for us or not, but they were in our direction so we just kept going as fast as we could motor away from land.

It took us more than a full 24 hours to reach the Treasury Islands at the north end of the Solomon's. There was a well-protected bay that I was familiar with when I had sailed to Bougainville Island from Gizo. I decided I could leave the boat there for as long as necessary so I could return to be with my brother.

When we arrived, we were surprised to see other boats anchored that we knew from the Kieta Yacht Club. I asked a young Australian couple to watch over my boat and my cat while I headed back to the States to be with my brother and my lady friend would head back to Australia.

We made our way to Gizo and both caught the first flight to Australia. I continued on to California where I spent several weeks with my brother until he passed away.

This was hard on my entire family. Depression set in like it had when Cindy's daughter had drowned in New Zealand. I never had any idea, when I was younger how hard it was to live with the death of someone you really love. More than anything, there is the feeling of guilt from something you had or had not done.

I still think about the arguments my brother and I had about pleading with him to stop smoking. To this day, I feel guilty for causing additional stress for my brother and my parents. I relive these memories almost daily.

My mom and dad took it even harder. We tried to talk about it, but it was too hard other than remembering all the good things about my brother.

While I was at my brother's, I kept in touch with my lady friend who told me she would like to sail with me for a while when I returned. Why not, I did not want to be alone now and the thought of sailing alone just after my brother's death did not appeal to me at all. She booked my flights back to Australia where we met and flew together to Honiara then to Gizo. Then we managed to hire a small boat to take us back to *Xiphias* in the Treasury Islands.

To my surprise, the young couple had taken excellent care of my cat and my boat while I was gone. In fact, they had moved aboard while we were gone because my boat was bigger than theirs and they enjoyed my cat.

We took *Xiphias* to Honiara for supplies, filled the fuel tank, and took on water. After a few days, we left for Port Moresby, the capital of Papua New Guinea.

We were about a day's sail from Port Moresby, sailing wing on wing downwind at about 6 knots in the middle of the night, when we hit a huge floating tree and got stuck in the branches. I immediately dropped the sails then attempted to push us off this huge tree.

It took many hours to free ourselves because the wind continued blowing us onto the tree and the prop was caught in the branches so I could not try to back us off with the motor. It was dark and I did not want to dive into the branches of the tree to attempt to free the prop. After hours of effort, we managed to push ourselves off the tree far enough that I could start the motor and back ourselves off the tree, and then continue sailing.

We arrived in Port Moresby safe and sound and put *Xiphias* in a marina for a week while we visited the city. There is much more to see in the interior of Papua New Guinea or on the islands. Port Moresby was just another large city. A week was more than enough time for us to see anything of interest.

One day, while we were visiting the city and returning to the boat, we could not find my cat. It was dark and I kept calling him but no answer. I was really beginning to think I had lost him, and I did not need this drama right now. I looked all over the marina then, just by chance, my flashlight showed he had dug his claws into the side of the walkway over the water. His eyes were closed, and I was not sure if he was still alive or not. I picked him up and he just laid in my hands, not moving. Then there was a little "meow" and some movement. I took him to the boat and dried him off. I had left plenty of food when we went to town and closed the doors, but I had left a porthole open for air. After crawling out through the open porthole he was simply checking things out when he must have fallen in the water.

Now it was time to leave for Darwin Australia. To get there we had to sail through the Torres Straits which were narrow, shallow, and full of coral reefs. This strait separates the Pacific Ocean from the Indian Ocean. The channel was well-marked with poles but hard to navigate at night because there were no lights in the straits. We managed to anchor a few nights behind coral atolls, of which there were many. We had a nice anchorage at our last atoll before we would reach Australian waters.

The next morning, when I tried to raise the anchor, it did not move. We had to move quickly because the tidal current was really strong, and I could only get my anchor up at slack tide. I put on my SCUBA gear and jumped into the water. I had less than an hour before the tide changed.

Fortunately, it was not too deep, and the water was crystal clear. My anchor chain had crossed over two large coral heads and slipped down between them. Then when I backed the boat down to set the anchor, it dragged under the huge coral heads. I could see I would have to re-anchor *Xiphias* in order to take the load off the anchor and get it free. After re-anchoring, I would have to pull the anchor back out the way it went in. By the time I surfaced the tide was changing so I had no choice but to cut the chain and leave this expensive, 45-pound CQR anchor where it was. Fortunately, I carried more anchors for storms and anchoring bow and stern.

We arrived at the Northern tip of Australia and began our sail across the Gulf of Carpentaria to Darwin. We stopped at several great anchorages and passed through some narrow channels, but it was a great sail. It took us several weeks because we were in no hurry. We were surprised at the number of huge crocodiles we saw while at anchor. I most certainly was not going to do any diving in these waters.

We anchored off the Darwin Yacht Club area which was not as easy as it sounds. There were high and low tide differences that control where you could and could not anchor. If you anchored too close to shore, then your boat may be aground at low tide and the bottom was not sand but soft mud. If you anchored out in deeper water, you cannot go ashore without walking in deep mud unless it was high tide. Many of the powerboats were anchored near the shore because it did not matter if they set in the mud at low tide. For the sailboats, they had to anchor in deeper water and control their coming and going ashore at or around high tide. There were too many times when I took our dinghy ashore at high tide but returned to find the tide going out and my dinghy set in the mud. I would have to walk in the soft mud pulling my dinghy behind me until I reached the water.

We spent a few weeks in Darwin, then we heard they were organizing a sailing race to Ambon Indonesia. This would be an easy way to get our visas for Indonesia.

Chapter 13
Back to Australia and on to Indonesia

Darwin, Australia where we enter the Darwin to Ambon, Indonesia race. Then we continue to Singapore. *We experience our first encounter with pirates that we had been warned about before leaving Darwin.*

I was getting *Xiphias* ready for the race. I wanted to put on my two-bladed prop instead of the three-bladed one I had on which caused too much drag under sail but more power when motoring. I set my two-bladed prop on the stern of my boat so I could reach it from the water.

I dove down and removed the three-bladed prop and set it on the transom when a guy yelled at me from a boat that had the Darwin Yacht Club name on it. He yelled out, "You crazy Yank, don't you realize these waters are filled with huge crocks? Get out of the water now!" I explained to him that there was no prop on my boat right now and I was trying to change it. Reluctantly, he agreed to stand watch for crocodiles while I put on my two-bladed prop. It was not easy for me to do because I kept looking over my shoulder expecting to see a crocodile at any time. Finally, I got it on without incident.

Our objective was not to win the race but to get our visas. At a meeting before the race, we were warned not to get out of sight of another boat because there were many pirates in the seas near Indonesia.

We left on our race and had a safe comfortable sail across the Timor Sea into the Banda Sea and arrived at Seram Island where Ambon was located. We did not spend a lot of time there because our visa time was limited so we left for Sulawesi across the Banda Sea.

Sulawesi had a huge bay but it was deep and not well-protected. I was told it was once a volcano. It was necessary to anchor parallel to the rocky shore. I anchored closer to shore than I would have liked because the land dropped off steeply into the deep. I used a bow and stern anchor to keep us from swinging ashore or dragging into deep water. The problem was the bottom was hard and it was difficult for the anchors to get a good hold, so I did not sleep at all that first night. For this reason, we only stayed two nights then continued toward Java across the Flores Sea into the Java Sea, and then on toward Singapore.

One day, as we were sailing off the huge island of Borneo, we saw a large, local pram type sailboat sailing at our speed not far to our starboard side, between us and Borneo. I slowed down and so did they. We began to worry because we had been warned of pirates in these waters. Then I saw a small uninhabited island ahead, to our port so we sailed around to the leeward side to anchor.

About two hours later, we saw the big pram sail into the anchorage. We were really worried now that they were pirates. I told my lady friend to go below and put on a hat, so she looked like a man. I took my flare gun and set it in the cockpit just in case. I could only stop one person and I was not sure if I wanted to attempt it. They sailed right up to our stern and one guy grabbed onto our backstay and started yelling something at me. I figured if he intended to board us, he would have already. We did not see any guns.

The other men behind him were making a circle shape with their hands. Then acted like they wanted to hit the inside of the circle. It appeared they were going to choke us and hit us on our heads. My friend said, "They want to strangle us." Since they did not attempt to come aboard, I was sure they were signaling about something round, maybe, with a handle. Yes, a bucket. I grabbed one from my side cockpit and they all smiled and gave me the "thumbs up" to signal that is what they wanted.

I passed it to the guy holding on to our boat and he passed it back to the others. I figured they were taking on water, so I began my search for another bucket when suddenly, the guy holding on to my backstay passed back my bucket, but it was full of king prawns. He smiled and shoved off and they sailed out of the anchorage. So much for pirates.

The next day we continued our sail into the Java sea towards Java. We wanted to do as much day sailing as we could and arrive in daylight. We left early in the morning and managed to anchor behind a small island on the way. The next day I decided to do a little snorkeling to see if I could spear some fish for dinner. As I was about to enter the water, my lady friend yelled out "shark" from the other side of the boat. I removed my fins and ran over there to see what she was yelling about. A huge Tiger shark was rubbing itself against the side of *Xiphias*. It was about 18 to 20 feet long. It passed around the stern and along the other side then rubbed against the boarding ladder I was going to use to enter and leave the water. That ended my snorkeling days for most of the rest of my life. I had come too close to being taken by this shark. What would have happened if I had entered the water only seconds earlier?

The next morning, we continued our sail toward Java. We continued past Bali and did not stop because my lady friend said she had been there, and it was just a tourist trap. After sailing for a few days, we arrived at the southern tip of Java. We found a small village that we felt would be safe for a night's sleep. To our surprise, we were immediately visited by some locals in a boat who signaled for us to come ashore. I tried to explain that we were tired and would come ashore the next morning.

Just after sunup and the morning prayer, we were visited by a local who was a teacher. He spoke poor English, but we understood him as he asked us to speak to his students. Apparently, we were the first foreign boat to arrive at their village. When we approached the shore, there were hundreds of people waiting for us.

After we pulled our dinghy onto the beach, we were surrounded by people who wanted to touch our hands, hair, and noses and stared into our eyes. It was apparent that we were the first white people they had seen for a long time or ever.

The teacher led us to his classroom where I began to speak slowly as he translated what I said. I tried to explain to these children that I was from the country where Disneyland was located. It was apparent neither they, nor their teacher, had any idea what I was talking about, so I tried to explain but I am sure they had never heard of Disneyland or Disney movies.

Then I tried to explain that we were from the other side of the earth. The teacher brought out a globe and I showed them Australia which was where my friend was from, and the United States which is where I was from. Now they knew I was an American and therefore had many questions I did not expect or understand. A lot of the questions appeared to be religious or about invading Iraq. We were asked if we liked Muslims. Of course, we liked all religions.

We spent three days anchored off this friendly little town and when it came time to leave, the whole village, including the students, came out to see us raise our anchor and leave. They stayed there waving until we were out of sight.

We were on our way to Singapore. We passed Lingga Island and Bintan Island to our port or left side and entered the bay at Bintan, our last anchorage in Indonesia before we would reach Singapore.

We just anchored for the night. It rained all night and when we raised our anchor, the rain was coming down so hard, I could not see but a few feet in front of me. I maintained a slow speed and compass course to get out when I saw a huge marker buoy. I decided to just circle around it, keeping it in sight until the rain let up. The heavy rain lasted for another 30 minutes before I could get back on my course.

Chapter 14
Singapore

Singapore is a country that is only a big modern city with everything a person could need. I needed work to earn some money to continue living my dream.

*W*e sailed across the Singapore Straits. There were anchored ships as far as the eye could see. There was no way a small boat like mine could anchor anywhere near those monsters. So, we headed for the channel to Changi where we heard there was a yacht club that welcomed foreign visitors.

We took a mooring and it was safe but the small, fast-moving commercial boats caused a lot of wake and rocked the boat violently day and night. However, we did not know where else to go for now.

After about a week, my lady friend decided to stay with me in Thailand. We both loved Singapore. The Metro train could take us anywhere we wanted for almost nothing. Then we could jump into a taxi. We found Singapore exceptionally clean. No debris in the streets. We heard there was a huge fine if you were caught throwing out your gum, the gum wrapper, or any trash. Thus, it got the nickname of a "Fine City."

The city was full of great, inexpensive restaurants. Some were big and fancy, but most were small. The food was excellent. I had my first experience eating fried cockroaches. Surprisingly, they tasted rather good and very crispy. They also had monkey brains on the menu but this one dish I could not try and there is not much that I wouldn't try.

I visited a local boatyard and met an American who ran the place. He asked me if I knew how to work on boats. I told him I did, and he put me to work the next day. He asked me to do some wood repairs on one of the boats to see if I knew what I was doing. After I had finished, he was impressed and said I had a job for as long as I wanted. The pay was not so good, but it did bring in some spending money and I was not in any hurry.

The boatyard was not far from the Changi Yacht Club. To get there I had to motor my small eight-foot dinghy up the Changi channel which separates Singapore from Malaysia. After a few weeks, I decided to move my boat closer to the boatyard so I could just row ashore and walk to work. However, I had a problem, the bottom was deep, soft mud and my anchor would not grab hold. I decided to take a vacant mooring they used to keep boats on before and after they finished working on them. I had to pay by the month.

One morning I went to work, and my friend went into the city to do some shopping. When I returned to the boat, it was not there, and then I saw it way down the channel. *Xiphias* had dragged about two hundred yards, dragging the mooring with it. Fortunately, it was down channel and nothing to hit.

It was time to set my mooring. I filled two 55-gallon drums with concrete and separated them about 20 feet apart with a heavy chain between them.

Then I connected a swivel in the center of the chain, between the two drums. I led my mooring line up from this swivel to a float that kept my mooring lines accessible. If the wind blew, it would have to drag the two drums together and cause a lot more resistance in the deep muddy bottom. This worked the entire time I was in Singapore.

We spent a considerable amount of time visiting the city, eating great food, and working. Then it was time to continue our sail to Thailand.

Chapter 15
Malaysia

Sailing the Malacca Straits on the Malaysian side which is a Muslim country that welcomes us with open arms. They broadcast their morning prayer at sunrise and the evening prayer at sunset. This was loud enough so that the whole town could hear. This was not the time to do anything but wait until the prayer ended. We stop and visit many places. I return home for a short time and my friend returns to Australia.

I do not remember how long we stayed in Singapore, but our visa was running out and we wanted to continue our cruising, so we took off early one morning and entered the Malacca Straits which separate Malaysia from Indonesia. The nice thing about sailing this Strait was that it was well-protected because there was land on both sides of the Straits. Sumatra of Indonesia was to our left and Malaysia to our right. We hugged the Malaysian side.

The center of the Straits was where the huge ships passed 24 hours a day and there were a lot of them every day. We hugged the Malaysia coast for the entire time we were in the Malacca Straits. When we did anchor near the shore, in shallow water, the ships would create huge wakes or waves that would cause *Xiphias* to rock violently keeping us awake most of the night. Also, we had been warned that there were pirates who would attempt to board and rob the ships, so we had to keep an eye out which also affected our sleep.

Our first really protected anchorage was in Port Klang. It was up a narrow channel. We finally reached the Royal Selangor Yacht Club where they gave us a mooring for as long as we wanted. The Yacht Club was a rich club with big, beautiful powerboats moored everywhere. This is where we officially checked into Malaysia. It was apparent that Malaysia was a Muslim country, but we were well-accepted. Women had to be careful not to show their legs or any part of their body.

We stuck around for nearly two weeks then continued sailing up the Straits. After a few more nights anchored near shore, we entered the area of Pangkor Island. There was a huge bay that was well-protected and a great anchorage. We spent several days there before we headed up the river to Lumut. We passed a Malaysian Naval base on our way.

Lumut had a small yacht club that permitted us to anchor near their moorings. The problem was that many large vessels, towing barges, passed by us heading up this river to other parts of Malaysia. This left a wake or wave of water that would violently rock the boats at all hours of the day or night.

The small Lumut Yacht Club was much more casual than any other yacht clubs we had visited. The Commodore spoke perfect English and welcomed us like we were locals. We liked it here and became too comfortable in this environment.

There were other cruising boats staying here. Some had left their boats to return to their home country for a short period of time. Others were in transit as we were. We made many friends with the other boat owners and the locals who came to the Lumut Yacht Club. On weekends we would take many of the locals out to the bay on Pangkor Island. They always brought lots of food and we had a great time anchored all day and talking about everything. They all spoke very good English.

My lady friend said she had to get back to Australia, so we took a bus to Kuala Lumpur, the capital of Malaysia, where she caught a plane home to Australia. I think that she had enough of living on a small boat. It was cramped and many times, uncomfortable. I totally understood her feelings.

I had anchored close to shore because of the traffic in the river. I had to set a bow and stern anchor because of the many severe squalls that came across the river and caused boats to drag. My bow was facing toward the river's center where the strong winds usually came from and the stern faced toward the shore.

One night there was a strong squall. I heard other boats blowing their horns and spotlights were everywhere. I got up to see who was dragging and saw nothing, but the spotlights were on me. I knew I was not dragging but started my engine just in case. I could see I was exactly where I originally anchored.

Then the spotlights hit a big barge full of dirt heading directly for me. It had been moored upriver and had apparently broken loose from its mooring in the strong winds. It was only a matter of one or two minutes before it would hit me.

I put the engine in reverse. Fortunately, I had stored all my stern anchor line and chain in a sail bag and had hung it over the starboard stern rail just in case I had to get away quickly. I released the stern line from the cleat and threw the bag overboard. Because of the chain inside the bag, it sank immediately. I left the engine in reverse as I ran forward and let all my chain run out to the end, which was attached to a small rope so I could not lose it. I kept a dive knife at the base of the mast for situations just like this.

I cut the rope and ran back to the cockpit. I increased the RPMs and shoved the tiller hard to starboard which moved the stern of *Xiphias* to port just as the barge passed where I had been anchored. The wind was blowing strong and the barge and I were both headed toward the rocks. I kept my engine in reverse until I was backed into safer waters. The barge hit the rocks.

Another boat yelled at me and waved me over. He permitted me to tie alongside until morning. This boat was on a mooring and I had no idea how strong it was, but the owner assured me it would hold us both. I had little choice; both of my primary anchors were on the bottom. I had two more small anchors, but they would never hold me in another squall.

The next morning, when it was calm, I dove for both my anchors and managed to get them both back on board. The barge was still sitting on the rocks. Then I decided to make a mooring, but not out of drums filled with concrete as I did in Singapore. Those hold a boat only by their weight. There was really no resistance to their design. Since they were round, they could drag.

Therefore, I designed another type. It was shaped like a pyramid with the top cut off. Since I would have to move this mooring where I wanted to set it with my own boat, I could not make it as big as I would like. So, I made two, which I would chain together after I had them both set where I wanted, like what I had done in Singapore.

I made a plywood mold. I found some old reinforcing steel rods and wired them together and put them inside this mold. Then I made a big, long, inverted "U" with "L" shaped ends that could be wired to the reinforcing steel. This is where I would connect the chain between the two moorings. Then I made a mound in the sand, placed a sheet of plastic over the mound then put the mold and steel on top of the plastic. Then all I had to do, was fill it with heavy rocks and concrete. The dome in the sand left the bottom of the mooring concave like the inside of an upside-down plate. This would permit it to settle into the bottom and cause a type of suction.

The objective of this mooring, being narrower at the top, was it could act as an anchor if it dragged, and the curved bottom would help prevent it from turning over. I planned to set the two of them about 15 feet apart and attached them with a heavy chain with a swivel in the middle. The top of the swivel is where I would connect my mooring chain that led to a float and then two mooring lines from the float to go to the boat.

I had to find some chain that would be strong enough, so I was looking for ½ inch chain. I went to the local Chinese hardware store where I found chain that would work. It was not a marine grade, but it did not matter. I was making the mooring to use for a short time.

When the worker went to cut the chain with big bolt cutters, he was going to cut the link where it is welded together. This would be much harder to cut than on the opposite side of the link. I tried to explain this to him, but he did not seem to understand so I showed him where I wanted the link cut.

When he cut the link opposite the side of the weld, the link broke into two pieces. The weld was not an actual weld but a surface weld about as thick as a piece of paper. I complained and he attempted to cut another link and the same thing happened.

I decided to find a marine hardware store and pay more money for some quality chain. One would never know this was bad chain just by looking at it. I felt fortunate to have insisted he cut the link on the opposite side of the weld.

I bought all the chain I needed and some shackles to attach the chain to the inverted "U" on top of each concrete pyramid.

At high tide, I managed to take each concrete block out to where I wanted them to sit. Then I dove down, in the dirty water and attached the chain between them and the swivel in the center of the chain. This worked perfectly for the months I was in Lumut. I would give it to the yacht club when I left.

There was a small boatyard upriver where they used two cranes to lift a boat out by using a sling around the bow with one crane and the stern with the other. They would lift the boat out of the water together and swing it over land. Then they would walk the boat to an area where they could set the boat on a cradle for as long as necessary.

I decided to go back to the States, my father was having heart problems and my mother asked me to come home. I did not want to leave my boat on my mooring while gone, not because of the mooring moving but because I did not want another barge or boat to break its mooring and come down on me when I was not there. So, I let another boat use it. I moved my boat to the boatyard and watched them walk it to a good location. It was supported with adjustable supports. I lashed them together and to the boat. I felt confident it would be OK while I was away.

I took a bus to Kuala Lumpur and caught a flight home. My father was not doing as badly as my mother had indicated or I had thought. Much of my father's problem was due to the fact that he was still having a hard time dealing with my brother's death. My brother was closer to our father, and I was closer to our mother. I don't know why, but that is how it was. If I were asked to choose one or the other, I could or would not be able to choose between them.

My father seemed OK, so after a month, I returned to *Xiphias*. I got a bus to the yacht club then a friend took me upriver where my boat was left sitting on the hard. It was dark and early in the night. I had to use a flashlight I'd brought with me. When I arrived. She looked just like I had left her only dirtier.

When I boarded her, I noticed there was a hole in the screen where I had a small porthole window. I had left the window open so air could circulate through the ceiling vent and the porthole. I had no idea why there was a hole in the screen until I went inside.

It was immediately apparent that there were rats aboard. I turned on the lights and saw they had entered my teak drawers and made nests in the drawers. To get out they gnawed a hole through the teak front which had a hole so your finger could pull it open. The cabin sole (floor) was full of rat droppings and pieces of debris. I could hear them running when I came below. My problem was it was late, and I was exhausted. I had to get some sleep before I attacked this problem. I poured myself a couple of strong scotches. The settee, where I normally slept, was clear of waste and debris, so I turned the sheet over and passed out.

In the middle of the night, I could hear them walking and running inside and outside the boat. I could even hear them scratch the side of the hull as they slid down the outside of the boat.

I could not sleep anymore. I was afraid they would jump into my bed. So I got up, turned on the lights, and saw a couple head forward into the chain locker. I got my fishnet out of a locker; that was used to lift the fish I caught out of the water and onto the boat.

I set it at one end of the chain locker hatch on the floor. When I lifted the hatch a few inches, two rats ran into the net. I was not thinking about anything but getting back to sleep, so I just stomped on them and set them aside to catch more. Within an hour I had caught and killed about eight. I threw the bodies over the side and went back to sleep.

The next morning, I explained what had happened to the owner of the yard and he gave me three, box-type traps but he warned that if the rats were afraid, they would not enter the traps to take the bait.

I tried them for a week and did not catch another rat, but I could still hear them at night. Eventually, I killed a few more, then I heard no more rats. I did a thorough cleaning, put *Xiphias* back in the water, and returned to Lumut.

I spent more time in Lumut before I decided to leave for Penang Island further up the Straits. It was a normal sail but about halfway there I saw a local fishing boat heading for me at high speed. I was worried that this could be a pirate. They came alongside and asked if I had any cigarettes. I told them I did not, and they threw me a good size fish and took off.

I anchored on the north side or lee side of Penang Island. It was only about 40-feet deep and my anchor took an immediate hold. When I went ashore, I had to check in with Immigration which is customary for every port in Malaysia. They asked me what I thought about the U.S. invading Iraq. This was in 1991 in an attempt to oust Saddam Hussein because he marched his troops into Kuwait.

I explained that I was a pacifist and did not believe in any kind of war. They seemed satisfied with my answer and signed my papers. As I walked through the town, I saw young men burning an American flag. I avoided this as much as I could. It was apparent that the Muslims did not like the idea of this war, or at least some didn't.

I really liked Penang because the town was modern, and the people were friendly to me. After about a week I went to raise my anchor and could not get it loose. It came up a bit, but it was like there was a spring pulling down on it. I put on my mask and fins and dove in to see what was causing the problem.

There, about 10 feet under the water I could see my anchor was fouled on a bunch of tires all connected by a chain. It was apparent they had made a man-made reef out of tires chained together. I returned aboard and gave it everything I had to lift the tires to the surface. When I did, it took me nearly an hour to hacksaw through the tire to free my anchor. Then I left for Langkawi, another big island that I heard had many nice anchorages.

It was only a full day's sail from Penang to Langkawi. The island was huge and had many smaller islands that I passed to enter the channel into the town. The interior of this island was well-protected with a sand bottom, perfect for anchoring. When I went ashore and reported to Immigration, I was, again, welcomed like a friend. In fact, I was invited to dinner at the home of one of the officers. They all spoke English and were great people.

Again, I could spend a lot of time in Langkawi. There were many anchorages. Some even had fresh water bubbling up from the ground near shore. This is where many of the local fishermen replenished their water supplies. There were a lot of local and cruising boats anchored all over the island.

I considered building a marina there and starting a yacht club. I rented a small motorcycle to search for a good location. I finally decided to make a turn and I did not see the car right behind me. He hit me and sent me flying. The only injury I had was all the skin torn off the side of my right foot from sliding down the paved road with my foot under the motorcycle. It exposed the raw flesh, but it was not too painful at the time.

The guy who hit me apologized profusely but I explained that it was my fault for not looking before turning. He offered to take me to a hospital, but I declined because I had to return this motorcycle. It was not severely damaged, and I could still ride it. The guy gave me a clean rag in which I could wrap my foot to protect it until I could get medical attention.

I rode back to where I had rented the motorcycle and offered to pay for the damage. The guy was nice and said he would settle for $50, which I knew would never cover the repairs. Then he insisted that he take me to the hospital. When we got there, the doctor wanted to do a skin graft from my butt or thigh, but I did not want two sores. I asked him to stitch it up the best he could which left a one and a half-inch round hole. He said it would heal but it could take a long time. This hospital bill was the equivalent of just US$3.00.

I was concerned because I had to walk in the water to get to and from my dinghy and to get it in and out of the water. These waters, even though salty, were full of filth. I was sure the town sewage entered these waters. The guy from the motorcycle rental place suggested I use a lot of Aloe Vera gel on it and keep it wrapped.

I did this and wrapped it in plastic when I had to walk in water. I always washed the area well and changed the bandage when I returned to my boat. It totally healed in about five months and today there is no scar at all. I am a firm believer in Aloe Vera gel to help heal large sores.

It was now time to head to Thailand. The border was not far from Langkawi and there were many islands where I could anchor along the way. I was heading for a huge, popular island named Phuket.

Chapter 16
Thailand

One of my favorite countries I have visited. I plan to return here to live after my cruising days are over. We ride elephants, a raft capsizes near the village of the Long Necks (women with golden rings around their necks to make their necks longer).

*M*y sail to Phuket was uneventful. They gave me a two-month visa and I had to take my boat out of the country before I could renew it. Phuket is a bit of a tourist place. Much more now than then. I met many of the locals and made some great friends. There was nothing about Phuket that I did not like.

One of my favorite places was Phang Nga Bay which is a huge bay full of small beautiful islands.

Some had caves in them where you could enter with your dinghy and look up at the stalagmites that looked like crystals. Several movies had been filmed in this beautiful bay.

There were some absolutely beautiful beaches that were fully protected from the weather. Many had young tourists sleeping in tents or cheap hotels. The view from the beach was something that you would expect to see in a movie.

I was in love with Phuket. There was nothing I did not like about it, except it did have a lot of tourists. I was sure this would be the number one place on my list to live when I can no longer cruise on my small boat.

I could have spent months there, but my visa was ready to expire so I left for Singapore where I would spend some time and then sail back to Phuket. I did this several times and sometimes I took a backpacker with me to share the expenses.

I met a fellow cruiser who owned a 40-foot sailboat. He had stripped out the interior and put in fold down pipe berths that could sleep about 12 people. He would put up ads in the hostels in Singapore looking for backpackers to pay to sail to Phuket, Thailand. He told me he only spent money on rice, potatoes, carrots, and canned tuna or chicken. There was bottled water and beer they could buy from him. They were not permitted to bring any food or drink aboard when they anchored, which was often. He told me he only did this non-stop during the dry season which was about eight months long. He also told me he was making about $50,000 a year after expenses. It was hard to believe but I know he was constantly going back and forth between Phuket and Singapore.

Once I took the bus to Bangkok and spent two weeks seeing all the sites. Simply a few weeks was not enough to see it all. I loved Bangkok and the tuk-tuk motorcycle taxis that would take you anywhere for almost nothing.

They have a food market where everything is sold including small boats. All these boats had long prop shafts that they used to power and steer the boat. The primary reason was that the water was shallow, and they could raise the prop, so it was just below the top of the water.

The town and surrounding area were filled with beautiful Buddhas of all shapes and sizes. There were huge Buddhas laying on their sides and one made of gold.

Then another time a friend of mine and I took a train to Chang Mai near the Burma (Myanmar) border. This place is famous for the different types of tours they offer. We decided to take one into the interior. We started as a group of six with one tour guide and a driver. We were driven into the interior. We were shown where they have large fields where they grow opium poppies. Then we had to walk through thick brush for about two miles when we arrived at a local village where people were living as they had a hundred years ago.

We slept on the floor on the inside of one of the locally built houses. They even managed to have a fire in the center of the wood floor in this wooden, grass house. We were offered opium to smoke. I declined but my friend tried it and got sick. We had to go outside to a group toilet when necessary. The people were not friendly at all. They accepted us but turned their heads when they saw us.

We rode on elephants for two days. One for each of us. I remember being on the neck of the elephant and its hair was like wire. It tore into the inside of my legs because I was wearing short pants. On the second day, they gave us all a blanket to put under us. We had two guides, one walked in front of us to lead the elephants and the other behind.

The path we were on was going up a hill and was getting narrower and narrower. The left side dropped way down into a gorge with a river at the bottom. The right side was a vertically steep mountain. It was so narrow it was apparent that two elephants could not pass each other, and it would be dangerous for one of these elephants to even turn around. It was not wide enough for a small car to drive one way on it. So, there was no turning back.

The road ended at the base of a steep incline. It was apparent these elephants had to climb. The first elephant placed one foot on the incline and pushed down until it held. Then another foot and slowly we all made it up this steep incline. I never had any idea that elephants could climb something this steep.

We reached a river where we were to leave our elephants and board a locally built raft made of bamboo, tied together with some kind of local twine. We were to get aboard one of these rafts and catch the current to take us to a village in Burma (Myanmar) where the Long Necks lived. This is where the women wear rings around their necks to make their necks longer.

The problem was the river was in flood stage. We had to sign a waiver if anything happened. They put our backpacks in a truck, they would not be going with us. There were two rafts for the six of us, and one person with a long pole to push us out into the current and attempt to control where we went.

This worked for the first hour then both rafts capsized on a curve in the strong current. Fortunately, we all could hold on to the raft, but it was almost impossible to get back on top without tipping it over again. After about half an hour or more, there was a bend in the river, and the guy who controlled the raft told us to start swimming toward shore.

We were met by some local men in loincloths who helped us out of the water. We were exhausted and wet but not cold, it was a warm day. We had to walk a short distance to a primitive-looking village. There we saw many women with numerous golden rings around their necks and some of their heads were about 10 inches above their shoulders.

Our guide told us that this custom began many years ago when a woman came to their village that had a long neck and several rings around her neck. The men all took to her and thus, thereafter, all the women tried to make their necks longer by placing rings around their necks starting at a young age.

We were permitted to spend a few days here. They let us stay in two separate homes. There were three of us in each house. While there, the men seemed to disappear, but the woman would play the guitar and attempt to sing something of their custom.

The rings the women wore around their necks were permanent and could not be removed. They were held in place by a single oval ring at the back of their neck. This oval ring could be removed to let the rings around their necks drop so they could clean their necks. The problem was that the neck had no muscles so the head would fall over and prevent them from breathing. They helped one another to support their heads by holding on to their hair as the back ring was removed and the rest of the rings dropped.

We were told that if a husband wants to, he can remove the ring in the back which would lead to the woman's death. We were also told that this custom of wearing neck rings is being stopped and the young girls do not have to wear these rings unless they want to. After a few days and nights in this village, the pick-up truck that had our backpacks showed up and drove us back into Thailand through a secret dirt road.

We returned to Chang Mai and I continued back to Phuket and *Xiphias*. After about a year of going back and forth between Singapore and Phuket, I decided to head for Sri Lanka.

I crossed the Andaman Sea and reached the Andaman and Nicobar Islands. Many were small and uninhabited providing perfect anchorages. Some were occupied but unfriendly. Not aggressive, just not friendly.

I was about 10 days out on the Indian Ocean approaching Sri Lanka when I got a radio message that my father had to have open-heart surgery and I was needed back home.

I considered continuing on to Sri Lanka, but I had heard that one does not want to leave their boat unattended for security reasons. It was also hard to catch flights back to the United States. It took me just over two weeks to sail back to Singapore where I flew home.

My father had already had his open-heart surgery by the time I got there but it was apparent that my mother and father needed me home. My cruising days were over, at least for now. When I returned to Singapore, I put *Xiphias* up for sale and it was sold within a few weeks.

Pintle and I flew back to the U.S. to be available to look after my parents.

Chapter 17
Back to California and the
Sam L. Morse Boat Building Co.

Family problems require I return home. I sell my boat, return to the U.S. and go to work for the builder of my Bristol Channel Cutter 28 and other Lyle Hess designed boats. After a few years, I am given the company because of the excessive debt it owed me. I build another Bristol Channel Cutter 28, Nereus from Greek mythology, "A Greek Sea God, known as The Old Man of the Sea, the son of Pontus." I run the company for a few more years and realize that I really need to return to cruising and go to Thailand before I get too much older.

*W*hen I returned home, I lived with my parents for a few months, but they seemed to be doing OK in their mid-80's. I had earned quite a bit of money working for the copper mine over the years, so I used some of it to pay off the mortgage they had on their home. This would give them a little more money so that they could live a bit more comfortably.

Sam L. Morse, the founder of the Sam L. Morse Company had passed away, and another person had bought the company from Sam's wife. The new owner had called my parents trying to find out how he could reach me. He was surprised that I was home, and he could talk to me directly. He wanted to know how I had designed my hard dodger and asked me to come visit him and discuss it.

I bought a commercial delivery van and converted the inside into a camper with a shower, stove, refrigerator, and a table that would convert into a bed. I decided to drive this van to Costa Mesa, California where the Sam L. Morse Company was located. This is the small company that had built *Xiphias*.

After I arrived, there was some discussion about my building knowledge and what I thought of the Bristol Channel Cutter. I told him a lot of things that should be changed like the mast was not as vertical as it should be which caused the boat to have too much weather helm (want to constantly turn into the wind). He asked me if I would work for him as a consultant at about $15 an hour to start. I could live in my van, so I decided why not. My parents were only a few hours' drive away and I had nothing else to do with my time.

After the first three months, it was apparent the company was broke. He could not pay me a cent, so he gave me IOUs. I did not realize it at the time, but these IOUs were useless unless they have a "pay by date." No "pay by date" then it never needs to be paid.

To keep the company open, I loaned it money. I got a receipt that said this made me part owner in the company. Then it happened again along with the IOU's. I finally had enough, and I told him to pay up or give me the company. I became the owner of the Sam L. Morse Company.

There was no money coming in or any boat orders, so I had to do some serious advertising in various magazines. This was not cheap but the only way we could find buyers. Several papers did a write up on the boats and their reputation. I was sure this would bring in customers.

Our company only had two full-time employees to build the boats, so it took a full year to finish one from start to finish. Crystaliner was contracted or paid to lay up the hull and deck for us and the two men did a great job of finishing it off.

There were no corners cut in building the Bristol Channel Cutter 28 or the Falmouth Cutter 22. They were built with thick, strong hulls and encapsulated lead ballasts. Everything was done to the highest standard possible and therefore these boats had a great reputation as "go-anywhere" boats. The problem was that this was an expensive way to build a boat.

I had to cut corners. I lived in my van. Fortunately, it was a small company that rented the space from Crystaliner who builds fiberglass powerboats. They seemed to keep busy building boats for the harbor patrol as well as fishing boats. They did high-quality work.

My two workmen went on unemployment, which had me worried that they might find work for another boatbuilding company if we did not get an order soon. I stayed in the office all day to answer the phone. I lived in my van at night.

I decided I had to do something to keep the company afloat. I decided to use more of my savings to build myself another boat. I missed sailing and it would put everyone back to work. Also, this would provide an opportunity for a potential buyer to see a boat in construction.

This would give me a place to live but not until the boat was finished in about a year. Since I could do everything at cost, I did everything I could think of to make her cruise ready.

Then, things began to pick up. I got one order that took away my worry about going broke for now. The new boat order took priority over my own boat. I moved out of my van and into my office. Then eventually, I rented a one-car garage from the previous owner who lived in Balboa, in the Newport Beach area of California.

It was small but slightly larger than my boat and a lot larger than my van. It had a small toilet, shower, stove, refrigerator, and a double bed. So for me, it was a luxury apartment.

Finally, my boat was finished so I could move aboard her and not pay the rent I was paying but I had to pay slip fees to keep the boat in a marina which, kind of balanced my accommodation expense.

When I could, I would sail *Nereus* out to Catalina and the outer islands on weekends. I felt back at home living aboard and sailing it as much as I could.

The company was just surviving but we were keeping our head above water. During this time, I tried to drive the 2+ hours to my parents on weekends when I did not sail. It was apparent my father's mind and health were getting worse. My mom was doing great, but she was in her mid-80's now.

Chapter 18
Looking After Elderly Parents

Elderly parents, nursing homes, and being a caregiver until the end. *After I sell the company, I return home to look after my parents. I watch my dad suffer from a failing mind and my mother suffers a horrible death.*

One day, while I was still working, my mom called me at work and said she could not live with my father anymore, he was just getting more violent.

I went home for a few days to see what I could do. I did not want to put him in a nursing home, so I started to look for a home care service where a person took clients into a house in order to look after them. Then I took my father to see the various homes that provided private care so he could choose the one he wanted. He chose the last one we looked at that only had women in the home. My dad wanted to live with all these women, and it looked like they wanted him to live there as well. He seemed happy when I left and returned to work.

This worked out for about six months, then the caregiver called me and said she could no longer look after him. She did not explain why but I knew it would happen sooner or later; my father's mind was not normal anymore. Reluctantly, I had to take him to a nursing home. There weren't many to choose from in Fresno at the time. When I found one, he seemed satisfied living there. He was not aware of what was happening.

I visited him and my mother every weekend. I called him regularly during the week to see if he was OK. One time he sounded like he was talking to me while underwater. It was apparent, he had liquid in his lungs. I asked him if there was anyone else in his room and he said a person was cleaning the floor. I asked to speak to this person, and I told this person to get a doctor to look at my father NOW.

I left for home immediately. He had pneumonia, which was later followed by a stroke. He passed away shortly after while in the hospital with my mother and me at his side.

Less than a year after my dad died, my mother while in her mid-80's was still driving and even had a boyfriend. I decided it was time to sell the Sam L. Morse Company and return to cruising. I was thinking my mother's new boyfriend would be there if necessary. I really wanted to return to  Phuket, Thailand to retire but knew I could not do it until after my mother passed away. I thought I would sail to Mexican waters and return home regularly to see how she was doing.

I had a Japanese friend who represented the company in Japan. He showed some interest in buying the company. We made a deal and the Sam L. Morse Co became his.

He soon discovered that they were expensive boats to build and there was little profit made when a boat is built to high standards. The high quality of work needed for these boats required the long-term employees to get paid a reasonable wage. They got paid better than I was able to pay myself when I owned the company.

He also lived a little better lifestyle than I had so the small profit that he did make was rapidly spent. After the first year, he had no choice but to raise the price of the boats. This basically took the boats off the market. A person could buy a much larger boat of a slightly lesser quality for the same price.

When cruising became popular, back in the late '60s, one of the most famous boats built was the Westsail 32. These boats, like the Bristol Channel Cutter, could cross oceans. Over the years, people started to want bigger boats that were of good quality, but the builders found cheaper methods of doing things that the builders of these smaller boats refused to do.

So as more and more boat builders developed, a person could buy a much larger boat for the same price as the smaller ones.

Unfortunately, he tried to sell the company but there were no buyers. He ended up selling the mold and rights to another boat builder in Canada to build the boat. So, the Sam L. Morse Co. no longer exists.

I sailed down the Baja coast of Mexico. I wanted to go home on Mother's Day to spend some time with my mother, so I put *Nereus* on the hard in La Paz, Mexico, and returned home, for what I thought would be a week or two.

When I got home, my mother told me that when her boyfriend discovered she was older than him, he left. Now she was alone, and I knew I would have to return home to be with her. I had only been home for about three days when she got pneumonia.

I hated the hospital where they had her because I suspected they were giving her the wrong medications, ones that were for someone else. I only discovered this by accident. My mother had a mild allergic reaction to certain medications, and some were bad for her heart. I had given the hospital a letter stating the medications that my mother was taking and those she had been advised not to take. One of the meds she should not take was there, on her list of medications to be given daily.

I wrote down the other medications she was being given according to her clipboard. When I got home, I googled these medications and they did not seem to have anything to do with my mother's pneumonia.

Some years earlier, my mother had a mild stroke that prevented her from smiling on one side of her mouth. It looked like that side of her face kind of drooped or had no muscle. She was given Coumadin to thin her blood to prevent another stroke. After nearly a year, her smile returned to normal, but she had to continue taking the blood thinners for life.

When I returned to the hospital the next morning, I was really upset. I raised hell and asked to speak to a doctor, but I was told I could not. I could only complain to the nurses. I asked the nurse why she was being given certain medications that did not seem to have anything to do with her problem and she was taking a medication that was on the list of drugs potentially dangerous for her.

The nurse took the clipboard to the front desk and hours later, returned with a new list of medications.

I wrote a strong letter to the hospital explaining what I had discovered. Shortly after, when I entered the hospital, I could hear the nurses say, "Look out, here comes that Mr. Olson."

Finally, my mother was released to a rehabilitation unit outside the hospital. My mother slowly got better but was far from being back to her normal self before the stroke.

After about two weeks in rehabilitation, they released her to me. I got a list of medications she was being given so I could continue giving them to her at home.

I reviewed the medications and noticed that her blood thinner medication was not on the list. So I asked them why. They told me that the blood thinner medication was not on the list of medications they were given from the hospital. I asked if she had been given any blood thinners while in their care. They said they are only allowed to give her the medications that the hospital provides.

I immediately kicked myself for not checking her medications while in the rehab center. I took her home and within five minutes after she sat down, she had another stroke and it started all over again, back to the hospital and rehab.

When I got her home, after the last rehabilitation, she was not able to do much of anything for herself; she needed 24-hour care. I refused to put her in a nursing home as I did with my father. I knew I had to be the one to take care of her.

The problem was that I had to move my boat to a different location because where I had left it was only temporary and the hurricane season was approaching. La Paz was a perfect target for a hurricane.

There were places on the mainland of Mexico that were safer where I could leave it as long as necessary. The problem was that I could not leave my mother.

I found a highly recommended caregiver to look after my mother for only two weeks so I could move my boat. I did not have much time, so I quickly moved *Nereus* from the Baja peninsula to the mainland where they had an excellent location to put a boat on the hard. It took me a week to get there. The place was called San Carlos, near Guaymas, Mexico. They had many boats standing on the hard that had survived past hurricanes. I did not get much sleep and I worked hard and fast to set her properly with plenty of supports. I felt comfortable leaving *Nereus* and took the first bus back to Arizona and flew home to be with my mother.

I looked after my mother 24/7 for the first year, then I knew I needed a break. I did not have a life, no going out except to buy groceries and medications. Even going for groceries was difficult because I had to leave my mother alone. She was unable to get out of bed on her own to go to the bathroom. She was not able to do much of anything but eat. I knew I had to hire a part-time caregiver. I looked in the papers and online for caregivers in Fresno.

I found a couple and asked for references. I was emailed two letters with excellent references and their phone numbers. I called and they verified that this person was good, so I hired her for a few days a week. It all seemed to go well but my mother did not like her. I thought the reason was because she was black. My mother and father were both a bit prejudiced. So, I ignored her complaints. When I felt more comfortable with the caregiver, I decided to take a few weeks off and go check out my boat and do a little work if necessary.

I took the train to Long Beach where I could stay on a friend's boat until I could board the train early the next morning for Arizona then take a bus to Mexico. That night, before I left Long Beach, I decided to call my mother at about 8:00 p.m. There was no answer. This was not right. After about ten tries I called the police and told them there was something wrong. I told them there was a live-in caregiver and she should answer the phone. They said they would keep me informed so I waited by the payphone.

Then I got a call back at about 10:00 p.m. They said the lights were on, but all the curtains were closed. They had knocked on the door but no answer. I told them where we hid the spare key so they could go inside to check on my mother. They found her on the floor. Our home phone was on the wall so after she fell, she could not reach it.

Apparently, the caregiver left my mother alone shortly after I left. My mother got hungry in the afternoon and tried to use her walker to get to the kitchen. She fell and was on the floor for about 10 hours. She was cold, upset, and semi-conscience. The police called an ambulance that took her to the hospital.

I canceled my trip and returned home as quickly as I could. I went to see her in the hospital. When I got there, they said they would release her after a few days.

I tried to find the caregiver without any luck. I filed a police report and they put out a warrant for her arrest. I called the people on the reference letters and discovered they were her daughters. They told me their mother had a drug problem and they thought she had quit. She wanted to work to keep herself busy, so they wrote the letters for her. Weeks led to months and nothing happened.

Then one of her daughters called me and said her mother was in jail for using drugs. I contacted the police department and told them they had her in lock up. They had no idea. I went to court to testify but it was not necessary, she had pleaded guilty to her offense against my mother. I did not care how long she was put away for only that she was found and would be in jail for a while.

I looked after my mother for more than a year. It was much harder than I thought. I had no life of my own. I tried doing some day trading in the stock market but that did not work because I would have to go care for my mother at a moment's notice. I would buy a stock at a low price, expecting it to go up. Then, to protect what I had paid for the stock, I set a lower limit to sell. This way I could not lose too much money if the stock price dropped when I was away from my computer.

Then my mother would call. I had to get her to the bathroom, then give her a shower, and make her breakfast before I could return to my computer. All too often, by that time, the stock had dropped to my sell limit and sold at a small loss then returned to its original price and went up from there. This happened too many times, so I finally gave up my day trading.

I hired a part-time caregiver but only left her alone with my mother when I went to buy groceries. She was a good and caring person. I really liked her, but I could never trust anyone to look after my mother long-term, nor would I put her in a nursing home. She was my responsibility.

One night my mother called out to me. She said she could not breathe, so I called an ambulance who took her back to the hospital. They told her and me, she had congestive heart failure and did not have long to live. They said she would be better off at home and they would provide a hospice worker to check on her twice a day. I took her home. The hospital sent over a hospice nurse who also brought a bottle of oxygen. She gave me some medications to give her when she had another episode of difficulty breathing.

About an hour after the hospice nurse left, my mother said she could not breathe and then brown foam started coming out of her mouth. I tried to give her the medication, she couldn't swallow it with the foam coming out of her mouth.

I cried out to God "please take her, do not make her suffer." I was terrified and crying, not knowing what to do. Then there was a knock on the door; I thought it was the nurse returning but it was a preacher who asked me if my mother would like to pray with him. To this day, I think it was God's way of answering my desperate prayer or plea for help to prevent my mother's suffering.

Soon as he saw my mother, he called the hospice nurse and told her this was not right. The nurse returned and gave her a shot and set her upright. My mother was no longer vomiting or coughing up foam, she seemed OK but was out like a light.

Then I yelled at the nurse why she gave me pills that I could not give my mother. She told me this situation was rare but when it happens, I should crush up the pills and put them under my mother's tongue. Why the hell didn't she tell me this before? I told her that I hated hospice and did not ever want them back. Before she left, my mother died not regaining consciousness. I still have a problem living with this in my mind. I still see it all so vividly

I find it difficult to talk about. I can write about it, but I am crying as I type the words.

I pray to God that I pass peacefully in my sleep or make myself die peacefully in my sleep.

This also makes me think about the way my brother and father died and compare it to the way my mother died. My brother was in horrible pain. I think he intentionally overdosed on Morphine that night. The reason I say this is that the hospice nurse made it a point for him to know that he was not to take more than the prescribed amount or it could kill him.

My father died not knowing one day from the next but he was in a coma and not aware of his surroundings. He was not even aware that he was dying. While my mother had full control of her thoughts and knew she was going to die soon. She was aware of everything that was happening.

Is it best to die not knowing what is happening or to die being totally aware that you are dying? We all know the answer, but can we choose?

I wonder how many people reading this have ever watched someone suffer a horrible death. Most people die in the hospital with constant medical drips and machines to prevent them from suffering. The problem with this is that the hospital bills will grow rapidly. Besides, most people prefer to die in their own homes with their families.

I remember a doctor who used to help terminal people die in peace in their own homes. He was put in prison for doing this.

We euthanize our pets to keep them from suffering, why not the people we love even more than our pets? I am not suggesting helping someone in good health to commit suicide. But is it wrong to help someone who knows they are going to die, to die in peace without suffering? I am certain that anyone who witnessed a loved one suffer before dying would agree that a person's request for euthanasia should be legal throughout the world.

I gave all my mother's stuff away to neighbors and the Goodwill. I had a memorial service where she and my father were cremated. My parents had paid in advance for this service and a place to keep their ashes. Then I had a memorial service in her home and only invited close friends and neighbors.

Chapter 19
Mexico to Panama

Now I need to get away from all the depression. The only place I feel comfortable and free is on my boat. I return to Nereus and sail south to Panama.

I sold the house and returned to *Nereus* on the hard near Guaymas, Mexico. I had a lot of work to do to get her ready to sail south. When finished, I invited my longtime friend to go with me, but he could not go all the way to Panama because he had his own business and could not be away that long. He suggested we take his son along too because he knew how to sail and he could continue on to Panama with me.

I had known his son since he was about fourteen years old. He was well into his twenties by now. I know he highly respected me and loved to sail with his father and me. This young man was a great sailor and totally reliable to stand his watches and do his share of the work while sailing. In fact, he dreamed of cruising just like I had done. This trip would give him more experience.

Our objective was not to get there quickly but to enjoy ourselves along the way. We worked our way down the Mexican coast, anchoring almost every night. We spent time in some beautiful areas and met other boats doing the same as we were. For the first time in years, I was beginning to feel normal and free again.

My friend, the young man's father, had to return to California when we entered Costa Rica. He had been good company, did his share of the sailing and standing watch. It was apparent that he enjoyed himself as much as I had.

I had another friend and his wife who wanted to join us, also for the experience, because they had bought a small boat like mine and were considering going cruising. They had friends in Costa Rica where they could stay until we arrived at Punta Arenas, Costa Rica. Then they would sail with us the short distance to Panama where they would return to Costa Rica before returning to the United States.

We took a mooring off the Yacht Club at Punta Arenas and waited for their arrival. When they arrived, they each had two huge suitcases and backpacks. I told them there was no room for those on my 28-foot boat with four people aboard. They managed to narrow it down to one large suitcase and a couple of backpacks and sent the others back with their friends. They would pick them up on their return from Panama.

Our sail south did not go so well. I kept giving my friends jobs to do so they could learn about cruising. There were a lot of necessary things to learn like setting the anchor or reefing the sails, etc. It was apparent that they did not have the aptitude for cruising. If the weather was a little bad, they would prefer to let my friend and I sail the boat and they would go inside to wait it out. We began having more conflict. I would have to repeat many of the instructions that they said I had not mentioned before. My young friend even tried to explain why this or that had to be done but they simply did not have the aptitude for cruising. By the time we got to Panama, there was little communication between us.

The cruising lifestyle is not easy no matter how many people are on board to help. One gets little sleep and must stay awake when standing watch at night. The weather often gets rough and sails must be reefed, changed, or dropped. One must gain experience slowly in all weather conditions because when you are out in the middle of the ocean, there is no one to call for help.

The only way to accomplish this is through experience. The more the better.

Chapter 20
The Republic of Panama

Panama takes me by surprise. I feel it is my second favorite place to live and retire. Panama not only has the Panama Canal, but it is politically safe, tropical, and no hurricanes or tornadoes. Many indigenous natives live like they did a hundred years ago but it is changing fast. Panama has a unique, controversial history.

We took a mooring at the Balboa Yacht Club. My two friends left the boat without a word of thanks or goodbye. It took some time, but we are still friends and keep in touch. They sold their boat and bought a recreational vehicle and drove throughout the United States. This was perfect for them because they really enjoyed themselves and met some great friends. Fortunately, they kept me posted on their travels.

My young friend and I decided to see some of the islands on the Pacific side of Panama before he returned home. We sailed out to the Las Perlas Islands and found many small islands and great anchorages.

Since Panama has up to 18-foot tides we had to be careful where we anchored. There had to be water under the keel at low tide and enough chain to hold us at high tide. There were times when we miscalculated and found ourselves sitting on the bottom. This was not a problem because the anchorages were well-protected, and few

waves could enter.

We would explore these uninhabited islands with our small dinghy and a 5 hp outboard. We found some beautiful beaches that totally disappeared at high tide. Because of these radical tides, there was a

lot of erosion that would remove some of the sand and turf from some of the tree roots.

We found the fishing great and there were rivers flowing down into some of the bays. This was a little dangerous because some of the tree branches, that overhung the river, had snakes sitting on them.

After a few weeks, we headed back to the Balboa Yacht Club, and my friend flew back to the States.

I really liked Panama. It was another unique country with native cultures that still live like they did a hundred years ago. It was apparent that their culture was changing though because many of the natives in the villages had cell phones.

There were the Wounaan and Embera tribes that were famous for their skill to carve large Tagua nuts into beautiful sculptures that looked like they were made of ivory. The artwork was almost perfect and they used natural colors to paint them. It is quite a sight when you see that they start with a large nut that looks like a rock.

Many villages did not have electricity, so it all had to be carved by hand. Sometimes they would glue or fuse two nuts together so the carving could be taller and more detailed.

We would sail or fly in a small plane to the Darien Jungle that borders Panama and Colombia. We would arrive in the small town of La Palma. If we sailed there, we would anchor off the small town. If we flew there, we stayed at the only hotel available. It was more than reasonable and exceptionally clean. ·

Many times, we would take *Nereus* up the river if it was deep enough. The problem was that, even though these were all freshwater rivers, they fed into the ocean, so the ocean's tides influenced the depth of the water. If the river was too shallow, we would take a small boat up a river to the small village where they weave, unbelievably beautifully designed baskets.

They would all gather with their pieces of art for us to choose from. It was difficult to decide because there were many and they were all cheap

The quality of these baskets was so good that many would even hold water. It must have taken them months to weave one of these beautiful pieces of art.

Unfortunately, most Panamanians did not feel the way I did because they did not sell as many as they should. Also, they would have to travel to Panama City to try to sell their work to the tourists.

I watched them weave some baskets. I was amazed at the way they fit in different colors and shapes as they wove. Depending on its size, it took them months to make just one.

All the Wounaan and Embera tribes lived next to freshwater rivers. Most of them were in the Darien Jungle. There were some closer to Panama City. These were a bit more touristy because they were much easier to get to than the ones in the Darien. We could make arrangements ahead of time for a group to go to one of these villages. They would meet us where we parked our cars. Then we would enter their boats and they would take us upriver to their village.

They were pretty much politically independent. Each village had a chief, like a Mayor who had a group of selected men who would decide on crimes and punishment if any was necessary. Rarely did any of these villages involve the Panamanian government even though, they were Panamanians.

Their homes were all set on stilts. They were made of local tree branches with coconut palm roofs. They had no ladders to use as stairs to enter. Instead, they carved notches into a tree log and leaned it against the raised floor to make a staircase.

I was impressed with their methods of construction. Apparently, one home would only last about 10 years, then it would have to be rebuilt. Lots of rain caused too much moisture which causes the wood to rot.

Another amazing thing I discovered was that they grew their own herbal medicinal plants. Plants that they swore would or could cure almost any disease.

They also had their own magic man, but it was not anywhere nearly as strongly believed in as in Papua New Guinea.

The Emberas had various reasons to celebrate by dancing. Sometimes it was just because they sold a lot of tagua or baskets. Other times it may be a wedding. Most recently they are doing it to attract more tourists.

Because I had visited the Wounaan and Embera villages in the Darien, which was the natural

way they lived, I noticed a big difference when I visited the ones closer to Panama. These were more to entertain the tourists. When there were no tourists around, the women would go topless. The men normally wore normal pants as we all do. Then when the tourists came, the women put their tops back on and the men got rid of their pants and wore their custom dress. When they danced their customary way, the women danced separately from the men but not always when there were tourists.

After visiting many of the land cultures we would fly to the Atlantic side and visit the Kuna Yala, actually spelled "Comaraca Guna Yala," a territory of the Republic of Panama. However, they are called "Kuna" by the locals. Like the Embera and Wounaan tribes, they have their own type of government and control of their own people.

They live on small islands on the Caribbean side. Each island is slightly different in size. Many are small, uninhabited islands where one would want to just sit or swim for hours.

Every island we visited was like an island a person would dream about if they were dreaming of tropical islands. They all had white sand beaches and colorful coconut palm trees. The water was clear and made skin diving on the reef a special experience.

However, those islands that were inhabited did not offer the same beautiful

treat. The homes were made of island wood and the roofs from the trees and palms on the island or the mainland jungle. Their toilets were out on the end of a small handmade pier and the waste went directly into the water.

The Kunas are famous for their hand-sewn Molas with beautiful colors and intricate designs that all had a meaning in their culture. These designs were originally tattooed on the women's stomach and back.

The missionaries convinced them to discontinue this tattoo habit. Instead, they should sew the design onto cloth and wear them on their front and back. At first, they were reluctant but eventually, this idea was accepted and all the Kuna women you see in Panama wear these sewn Molas.

Molas are sewn entirely by hand. They put four layers of different colored cloth together. Then they draw their design. The line is cut, and the edges tucked under exposing the different colored material below, they are then sewn by hand.

Difficult and intricate sewing are required. The more detailed the design, the more work is required.

All molas, like their original tattoos, are "slightly" different from the front and back but of the same design. The difference is hard to see.

It seems impossible that they can make some of them so perfect and all done by hand, no machine of any kind is used. The missionaries brought them a bunch of sewing machines, but the Kuna preferred to sew them by hand. By hand, they could be much more intricate with their design.

There are now "tourist" molas, like a fish or bird that only takes a short time to make. If you compare one of the "tourist" molas to the originally designed molas that have a meaning in their culture, you can see the difference.

An original mola is exquisitely designed and intricate but different in the front and back. If you look closely at these two molas of a turtle, you can see they are the same design. But look closely at the color of the lines. You will see some of the lines are of different colors, but you really must compare each section. As an example, look in the center of each turtle's back and see the difference. You will see that some of the lines are of a different color. One mola goes on the front and the other on the back of the Kuna woman.

The Kuna people originated in Colombia. Then there was a war between the Kuna and the Embera tribes. The Kuna moved north into what is now known as Panama. The Wounaan and

Embera followed, still fighting, forcing the Kuna to move off the land, out onto the islands of the Caribbean side.

There is a great history of the Kuna that few people know about. I only know about it because I became good friends with a young Kuna man who took the time to explain in detail the customs they practice today and what it all means. Everything they wear has a purpose from their history but that is all slowly changing.

An interesting fact about the Kuna is they are a matriarchal society (a society controlled by women). This means that everything belongs to the women. You would not know this normally, but it is still true today.

All adult women have short hair. Girls, from their youth, do not cut their hair until they begin their "Menarche" (from Greek, meaning beginning and monthly) or menstrual cycle. This is when a woman reaches puberty and it is the beginning of fertility.

On this first day, they have a "hair cutting ceremony" that goes on for days or as long as the "period" lasts. The young girls are enclosed in their rooms and bathed constantly by their mother or other women of the village, no men. Meanwhile, the rest of the village celebrates by getting drunk on fermented coconut water. The drunker they get the more it shows their respect for the girl. Then they cut her hair short and it remains cut short for the rest of her life. I was fortunate to attend one of these celebrations and I did get drunk.

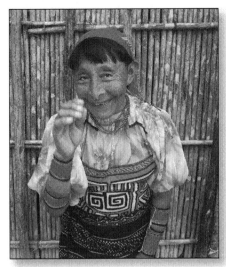

All Kuna women wear colorful beads around their ankles to their calves. These beads represent the earth where each Kuna originates. All Kuna originally came from the earth.

The gold rings the women wear in their noses are there to keep evil spirits away. There are so many more stories like this about their original customs.

Unfortunately, these tribes are slowly losing their ancient customs and beliefs because they are being exposed to television and cell phones. I wonder how much longer they will all be so unique.

Panama is also unique because of the Panama Canal which connects the Pacific to the Atlantic so ships can pass from one side to the other without having to go around Cape Horn in South America. It has a long history.

The Canal was started by the French in 1870. They found it too difficult, so the Americans took over. The biggest problem was Malaria and Yellow Fever. Too many workmen got ill, and many died. Eventually, they got malaria under control and were able to finish the Canal in 1914.

During the latter years of building the Canal, the Americans brought over a large military force. There was a time when there were more American military in Panama than anywhere else in the world.

The Americans had a huge military presence mainly to protect the Panama Canal from any foreign intervention. There were six military bases on the Pacific side and five bases on the Atlantic side. There were many areas where there was no military but there was housing for the people who were here for the Canal. Panamanians had free access to these areas but not the military bases.

They built homes for all their military personnel. The lower ranks stayed in barracks while those of higher rank got duplexes.

The highest-ranking officers were given large, 3-story homes. These homes still exist mostly in the Albrook and Clayton areas of Panama.

Everywhere, near the canal zone, buildings still exist that were built by the Americans for their military use or as military residences.

There are still a lot of Americans living here from those days. They call them "Zonians" because they lived in the American Canal Zone.

Panama also has a great history that is too complicated to explain here, but I would like to mention a few because it shows a lot of conflict between Panama and the United States.

One of the events is called "Martyr's Day of Mourning." Back on January 9, 1964, there were both American and Panamanian flags being flown in the American controlled "Canal Zone." This was decreed by President John F. Kennedy but never actually went into effect because he was assassinated shortly after this decree. As a result, the governor of the American Canal Zone said that all flags would be removed except in American military and government areas. Schools were to have no flags.

At an American high school in Balboa, the students and a few adults decided they would fly the American flag. The Panamanian flag was not being flown. Some Panamanian students from a nearby Panamanian high school decided they were going to protest. So, a group of Panamanian youths and some adults decided to march on the Balboa school and raise their flag alongside the American flag. The serious part was that this Panamanian flag was a famous flag from 1946 that had a lot of Panamanian history.

There was a lot of confrontation in their attempt and the American Canal Zone police were attempting to stop this from happening. The result was the historic Panamanian flag was torn, nearly into shreds. This resulted in many Panamanians getting angry. Thus, protests began all over Panama City and inside the American Canal Zone that lasted for weeks.

From here there is a lot of controversy about what happened that resulted in 22 Panamanians being killed, along with four Americans. This holiday is celebrated on January 9th each year.

Another major event that happened, more recently, was "Operation Just Cause" by President George H. W. Bush. This is when the American military attacked Panama on December 20, 1989. The reason for the attack was to remove Panama's President, Manuel Noriega.

Before this occurred, Manual Noriega was the head military officer for President Omar Torrijos who, they claim, was a dictator. Strangely, Omar Torrijos died in a plane crash during takeoff from Panama City in 1981. Then Florencio Flores Aguilar took over as President. Almost immediately, Noriega staged a military coup against him and he took over. At the time, it was public knowledge that Panama was a hub for drug trafficking, using Panama to transfer drugs between Colombia and the States.

Noriega worked for the American CIA to help stop this from happening. Noriega, early on in his career, quickly learned that there was more to be gained by helping move the drugs than stopping it. So, he told the United States CIA to shove it.

How this attack was carried out is where the controversy begins. What happened is very controversial, depending on if you are speaking to a "Zonian" or a Panamanian who was directly involved. Also, there are controversial news stories and videos that exist that do not paint a pretty picture of the attack and what hit the American media. Many Panamanian citizens were killed, lost their homes and jobs. Even today, there are many Panamanians who hate Americans and others that thank them. There are videos from various news outlets interviewing Panamanian residents about why they were forced out of their homes and forced to live in a military airplane hangar along with hundreds of other Panamanians until the war was over.

There is also the story of a group of Panamanian Military who arrested Noriega and wanted to turn him over to the American forces. All they asked, was not to let the Panamanian Military enter where they held Noriega. The Americans did not do this, and the Panamanian Military entered the facility to rescue Noriega and kill the men who had arrested him.

I still discuss some of these events with Panamanians and "Zonians" that were here at the time and get their different views. I have watched videos of the attack and interviews with the Panamanians and now totally understand why there is so much controversy about "Operation Just Cause." I have no idea what really happened, and I am glad I was not here to witness it.

In 1977, President Jimmy Carter signed an agreement to turn the Panama Canal over to the Panamanians by the year 2000. This happened on December 31, 1999, and all American military left Panama. However, many of the American families who were raised and lived here stayed. Today those people are called "Zonians."

Today, Panama is not permitted to have a military force because the United States, promised to guard Panama and the Panama Canal against any possible threats.

Because people from all over the world were brought to Panama to help build the canal, the country is totally diversified with every kind of race and religion. There is not, nor has there ever been, to my knowledge, any kind of protest or violence for racial or religious reasons, unlike the U.S.

The national language of Panama is Spanish, but as my Colombian wife would say, "It is Panamanian Spanish." There are many who speak English because there are so many "Zonians" still living here. As such, I find this the perfect place to retire. The medical doctors and services are excellent and reasonably priced. Not cheap but less than half what one would pay in the U.S.

There is only one problem; they do not accept Medicare here but that is the fault of the United States, not Panama. They do accept many U.S. medical insurances if the insurance company permits it.

As my last comment on the subject: PANAMA DOES NOT HAVE ANY HURRICANES OR TORNADOES.

Chapter 21
The Adventure Comes to an End with Marriage

I marry a woman who does not speak a word of English, so I must learn to speak Spanish. This is a new experience; living with someone with whom I cannot clearly communicate. It is most difficult but it improves daily.

One evening, at the Balboa Yacht Club restaurant, I met a couple of "Zonians." They invited me to have dinner at their condo in Albrook where the American Military used to reside. They picked me up and took me to a brand-new complex with over a hundred apartments/condos. The complex had been built from the original American military barracks. They had torn down the old barracks, kept the structural supports, and built a new four-level complex. The apartment/condo was small, only about 861 square feet. This included two bedrooms, two bathrooms with showers, a medium-sized kitchen, a small dining area, and a small living room. It was just the right size for me, after living so many years on a 28-foot sailboat. There were still some units available and the price was right. I bought one, with the plan to continue to cruise and hoped to rent my place while I was gone. Even better yet, I had a place to come back to when I was ready if I wanted. I looked at it as an investment.

Since it was brand new, it required a lot of work like ceiling lights, ceiling fans, painting, refrigerator, stove, furniture, air conditioner, etc. But I enjoyed doing it and having a place I liked in Panama. I temporarily moved off *Nereus* and moved into the apartment. It was a secure complex with a security guard at the entrance and, of course, an administration fee to pay for maintenance and security but it was very reasonable. I became good friends with the couple who had invited me to dinner. They lived just one floor below me.

This is where I met my wife. She was in the office, running the administration of the complex. She was cute, a little younger than I but only spoke Spanish, and my Spanish was far from fluent or even good. As the months passed, I studied Spanish and kept asking her out, but she said "no" because I did not speak Spanish. Then late one afternoon, she called me and asked if I liked Colombian coffee (she was from Colombia). I said sure and she brought up a bag of Juan Valdez coffee. This was the beginning of our relationship.

After months of dating, we ended up living together for about a year. I put off my desire to continuing cruising. After all, I was now sixty-five. Then the time came for her to renew her working visa. Somehow, her boss had not renewed it because her lawyer had told her it was not necessary because she was family. So now Gladys had extended past her working visa status. We met with my lawyer and she told us that Gladys had broken the law. She would be deported back to Colombia and probably not be permitted to return to Panama. The only solution was to get married, which I swore I would never do again after the divorce of my first wife. I really cared for Gladys and did not want to lose her, so I asked her to marry me and she said yes. This was her first marriage and neither of us had any children which made it perfect for both of us. We went to a judge and got married. My friends were our witnesses and Gladys' parents had flown in from Colombia to be at our wedding.

My wife, Gladys, comes from a big family with seven brothers and sisters for a total of eight. I have met them all including aunts, uncles, nephews, nieces, etc and they are really great, caring people who are smart and full of love and affection for all people of this world. I feel so fortunate that I married a woman with a family that will always be there for her, or for me for that matter.

The ceremony was nothing special, but we were married. As I write this, we have been married for 15 years and I have no regrets.

The biggest problem with our marriage was that she did not speak a word of English and my Spanish was far from fluent. I studied Spanish on my own then hired a person to teach me Spanish. After all these years I came to realize that learning a language when you get old is difficult to impossible. We could communicate if she spoke slowly. Since she is from Colombia, her Spanish is a clear form of Spanish like the type I learned in high school or through books and recording tapes. Panamanian Spanish is really hard for me to understand. Mostly because it has a different accent and they talk too fast for me to understand.

My wife even has problems understanding Panamanians sometimes. When we go out, I tell my wife I want to practice so let me do the talking. I ask them to speak slowly because my Spanish is not that good. They will start speaking slowly, then when they can see I understand, they speed up and I get lost. I turn to Gladys who must take over and translate for me. It is interesting because she is not translating from Spanish to English but from Panamanian Spanish to Colombian Spanish. I love to see the expression of local Panamanians as they listen to my wife repeating what they said to me in Spanish.

Our communication is not at the level I would prefer. I cannot discuss philosophy or other more complicated subjects with her. The biggest problem is when we get into an argument, Gladys speaks too fast when she is mad. There is no way I can understand or respond so I simply agree, "Si mi amor, si mi amor." This ends the argument. She got her way, so she is happy. Nothing changes, so apparently the argument was not important anyway. Life is too short to fight with one's wife unless it has to do with something important. When it is something important, she will speak slowly to make sure I understand, and we always resolve our problem.

People think that it was easy for me to learn Spanish since I live with someone who only speaks Spanish. What they do not realize is that if I have a question about how to use a word, I must ask it in my bad Spanish. She cannot explain it to me in English. For all our years together, I have paid tutors which got expensive. I decided I had to learn it on my own. I know many words, but putting them in the correct order or use special tenses is nearly impossible for me. I study a little each day, but I am still far from fluent and I now realize, I never will be...at my age. To learn a language is for younger people or at least younger than me. Up to the date of this writing, my wife does not know one word of English. We live in Panama so there is no reason for her to learn.

Gladys and I sailed out to the Las Perlas islands several times and visited the various tribes in Panama. It became apparent that my wife did not like sailing. It was not only the fact that she couldn't swim but she got seasick as well. After a few years, I decided to sell *Nereus*. It was apparent that I was not going cruising anymore.

I had no trouble selling her to a doctor who lived in Texas. However, he said that there was one condition, I had to deliver it to Galveston, Texas. That sounded great to me! My last chance to really do some cruising, and this time in the Caribbean.

A longtime friend from California, flew to Panama to help me deliver the boat. We had to transit the Panama Canal to get to the Atlantic side. Then we had to wait for over a week because the weather was bad. We were running out of time, so we left in rough weather. It was rough for a few days but nothing like what I had experienced when I was cruising.

After the first five days, our sail was easy with just the right amount of wind to keep us sailing at a good speed and the seas were rather calm. We spent time at various islands to replenish supplies and act like tourists. The objective was to try and enjoy this delivery and still get the boat there safely. The new owner had no objection at all. All he wanted was his boat delivered to Galveston safe and sound.

Over the years, I bought other boats, fixed them up, and sailed them around Panama. I was fortunate to always sell them for more than I had paid, but it was still about break even when you consider the amount of money and work I put into each boat.

Cruising was and still is in my blood. However, my age tells me I am too old to even consider returning to the sea. I feel so fortunate for what I have done, thus the writing of this story.

Conclusion

*B*efore I begin my conclusion, I would like to mention that I have spent many hours making any single decision that could affect my or someone else's life. This is not an easy task because you must remember that there is not always a right or wrong decision but whatever it is, it may have a positive or negative effect on the rest of your life. Sometimes I will write down on a piece of paper all the items I should consider, positive and negative. Then I make a value from 1 to 10 on its importance in making my decision. Everything you can think of must be noted. This will not happen in an hour or two, but it will take days as possibilities enter your mind. When finished, add up the points to see which one has the most advantages. If the result is not what you expected or wanted, then take the path you feel is right. At least you know you seriously attempted to make the right decision.

If the reader was impressed with my life's story and considering doing something similar. I would like to emphasize that it is not as easy and as simple as I may have made it sound. I have left out a lot because it is too technical for a person who is not an experienced sailor. I have also left out the details of the many mistakes I made but they all became a learning experience.

This type of lifestyle is full of the "unexpected." There are weather conditions that cannot be avoided. A watch should be stood 24-hours a day because of ships and other dangers that may not be seen until it is too late. When I sailed alone, I set a cooking alarm for every 15 minutes to 30 minutes, depending on the kind of waters in which I was sailing. If I were in the major shipping lanes or where there was the possibility of reefs, I would set it for 15 minutes. If on the open ocean with nothing on the horizon or in my way, I set it for 30 minutes. I sat outside, when the alarm goes off, I look 360 degrees around then I reset the alarm and go back to sleep. This goes on all night and even into the day until I feel rested.

There are ocean bottoms that do not permit an anchor to be set securely. There are various anchor types for various situations. Carry a minimum of three anchors of different types. Even more may come in handy, depending on the size of your boat.

There are areas where you feel you must anchor to get some rest, but it is a coral bottom or too deep. It is advisable to avoid anchoring in coral.

The locals will think you are rich because you are sailing so far from home, so they may attempt to board your boat while you are aboard or while you are ashore. Then there are health conditions or accidents that suddenly happen which you have no control to prevent. Have a comprehensive first aid kit that includes lidocaine for injection so you can do minor surgery on yourself or someone else. This includes a sharp scalpel and plenty of antibiotic ointment and alcohol. I had to use it three times and I was so thankful I had it.

As for the boat, larger is not necessarily better. Good quality construction should take priority over size and speed. The cruising lifestyle can be as expensive as you let it be.

If you feel like you want to do something like I did, you must gain experience. When the weather turns bad and all the other boats are coming in, this is the time to go out and practice your storm strategy so you can do it without even thinking about it. You may not have the time to ponder on your strategy or think you can make it to a safe anchorage. There are many storm strategies that one should learn, depending on the severity of the storm.

Practice anchoring in as many various areas and situations as you can. Learn to set two anchors off the bow and one off the stern. This sounds easier than it is, depending on the weather conditions. You also need to be prepared for the unexpected so have a strategy where you can quickly cast off both bow and stern lines as quickly as possible.

Never, totally rely on the engine. It will often fail to start or there may be something caught in the prop at the worst possible time. Which brings up the point, you should know everything you can about your engine and the electronics you have aboard. One common mistake many sailors make it they let the fuel in the fuel tank get too low. If the boat is motoring in rough seas to get to safety, the fuel line may suck up a bit of air that will stall the engine. This has caused many disasters.

Also, consider what you are missing back home. Many cruisers begin after retirement because of a lack of funds. Keep this in mind when making the decision. Are you too old or in poor health? I know of many boats that intended to cruise the world. By the time they reach Panama, there is a health or family problem that requires them to return home. Their boats are often abandoned here in Panama to eventually sink, or the government takes possession.

I am often asked how I could afford to live such a life. I explain that a person can live how they want to live. Do you really need that big of a home? Do you really have to go so far in debt? For me, I left with only $10,000 to my name. That was from my retirement fund after teaching for 15 years. I found work on boats and construction along my way. I always saved as much as I could and never spent money on anything that was not necessary. Maybe a book or two. So, my success has been being skilled with my hands and saving more than I spend. When I did make some money, like selling a boat or my business, the money went into savings and interest-bearing stocks. This is how I live today but I can no longer work...so I write...

I considered writing about carrying guns aboard your boat. Just be aware that most countries will confiscate your weapon if they find it. From my experience, too many people have guns that do not know when to use them. I have many more stories about boats with guns. The decision to carry a gun aboard is personal, so I will not make any further comments on it.

I could continue this but the bottom line is: "If you know what you are doing, then live your dream. It is worth it."

Amazon sells one of my books that is more about "how to prepare for a cruise" than it is a story about cruising. It is titled: "PLOT YOUR COURSE TO ADVENTURE. How to be a successful cruiser." There are many other books that one should read before attempting to live this type of lifestyle.

Actual Names of Those to Whom I Feel Indebted

The following is a list of names of people to whom I feel I owe gratitude because they had a positive influence on my life. Because of them, I am proud to be who I am today. Forgive me if I misspelled your name. I have had many good friends that may not be mentioned. That does not mean anything negative, simply our friendship did not affect me as strongly as those mentioned below. I have had many excellent friends throughout my life. Thank you to all I have met throughout my life. There are some who I cannot even remember their names so please forgive me.

This list is not alphabetical but instead, chronological from my youth to today. I also listed the location and the approximate year.

Ronnie Atkins, Dos Palos, CA, 1940's

Bill Courant, Dos Palos, CA, 1950's

Archie Swindle, Dos Palos, CA, 1950's

John Vaught, Dos Palos, CA, 1950's

Johnny Ronquillo, Dos Palos, CA, 1950's

Jerry Whitworth, Navy, 1957 to today

Stan Crawford, 1960's to today

Nobe Watenabe, Fresno California State College, 1960's

Owner and fellow employee at Shakey's Pizza Parlor, Fresno, CA, 1960's

Sam Sincher, fellow teacher, La Puente High School, CA, 1960's

Sam L. Morse, Owner of the company who built my boat, 1970's

Bob Pearson, Long Beach, CA. 1970's

Lyle Hess, Designer, and friend who designed my boat, 1970's

Cindy, Ashley, and Chris, 1978 to forever in my mind

Lynn and Larry Pardey, 1970's to now

Mike Anderson, "Freehand Steering," 1970's to now

Charlie and Nita "Mintaka" Pacific Ocean, 1980's

Joe and Opeta, Natives of Papeete, Tahiti, French Polynesia, 1980's

John Woods, Keri Keri, New Zealand, 1980's

Keith and Angela, New Zealand, 1980's

Wendy Mansel, Australia, Papua New Guinea, 1980's

Doug Laird, Australia, Papua New Guinea, 1980's to today

Lindsey Lang, Papua New Guinea, Australia, 1980's to today

Betty Pearce, Sailing and lectures together 1970s +

Bill and Jeanette Jones, Papua New Guinea, Australia, Costa Rica, 1980's to today

Herb and Margo Callaghan, Papua New Guinea, Panama, 1980's to today

Manny and Roz Liarriturri, California, 1990's to today

Michael Cochran, San Francisco Bay area, 1990's to today

Lokke Patrick, Long Beach, California, 1990's to today

Tim Patrick, Long Beach, California, 1990's to today

Marcela Somolova, Czech Republic, California, Panama, 1990' to today

Rex Jensen, Panama City, Panama, 2000's to today

Ed Wardlow, Albrook, Panama, 2000's to today

Vicki Seizemore, Albrook, Panama, 2000's to today

Carmenza Spadafora, Albrook, Panama, 2000's

Paul Kaiser, Clayton, Panama 2000's to today

Roberto Irazabal, Abrook, Panama, 2000's to today

About the Author

R oger Olson was born in 1939 in the small town of Dos Palos, California. In his youth, he would drive to the coast and SCUBA dive. He spent time looking over the horizon, dreaming that one day he would find out what was on the other side.

After serving in the military, he went to college to get his master's degree in Secondary Education. He got married and taught at La Puente High School in California for 15 years. A sudden, unexpected divorce changed his life and made him take stock of his goals and direction.

He decided that he wanted to fulfill his lifelong dream of going off over the horizon. But to do that he had to learn how to sail. While learning to sail and maintain ocean-going sailboats, he owned several sailboats. After sailing much of the Pacific Coast and Baja, Mexico he concluded that the size and speed of a vessel were not as important as strength and the ability to handle all sea conditions.

He did not want to sail around the world. He wanted to visit as many countries and islands as possible. He wanted to spend as much time as necessary so he could learn as much as he could about other cultures. He lived as cheaply as possible and found local work at some of the places he visited. He found that a great way to learn about a culture is by working with its people.

His life as a cruising sailor was marked with much wonderment, and occasional deep tragedy and loss.

After visiting many Pacific Islands and countries, he continued to Melanesia, Malaysia, Indonesia, Singapore, and Thailand. After many years he had to return home to look after elderly parents, but this did not change his desire to live his dream. After his parents died, he intended to return to Thailand and continue from there. But, when he reached Panama, he fell in love with that small country with its many various cultures. Considering his age, he decided to settle down but still live his dream in Panama.

Printed in Great Britain
by Amazon

21532376R10111